Adopting a Musical Approach

By Cat McGill

"Cat's fabulous music and accompanying guide will be helpful to therapeutic parents who want to explore fresh and enjoyable ways to connect with their child and ease them through the day with a song and a smile."

— Sally Donovan, award-winning author of *The Unofficial Guide to Adoptive Parenting* and *No Matter What.*

ADOPTING A MUSICAL APPROACH

First edition. July 2019

For my children:
I will love you.

CAT McGILL

Contents

Introduction

Hello! Welcome to *Adopting a Musical Approach*! I'm Cat, a singer and musician, and mum to two children. Fairy (not her real name!) is my birth daughter, she's nearly twelve and she's autistic, like me. Tickle is adopted; he's coming up for ten although he's still quite delayed in some areas. He's been living with us for around four years, and it's been incredibly tough and an absolute privilege all at once.

This is going to sound like a bit of an odd way to introduce a book, but I actually never intended to write this one at all. *AAMA* originally was a songwriting project, so the plan was always to do an album, and jot down a few thoughts in the sleeve notes about what I'd learned along the way. However, it all snowballed a bit, as these things tend to do, and it became pretty clear that there was more I wanted to share with you than I was going to be able to pack in to the sleeve notes, even if I made the text really small! (If you've stumbled across this book in some other way, you may not have realised that there is an accompanying CD, and although you're perfectly welcome to read the book without listening to the songs, it is intended to go hand in hand with the album. If you're not sure where to get a copy, have a look at my website: catmcgill.uk.)

AAMA was conceived as a project to explore how I could create music that could help adoptive, fostering, and special guardianship families, and in particular the children in those families who have experienced the care system. My day job is as a musician and singer, and I often work with people who have profound and multiple learning disabilities, using music to communicate and interact with them. Music is a powerful tool for connecting with people, and I wanted to take my experience of using music in a therapeutic way, and apply it to what I know about adoption and trauma.

CAT McGILL

My starting point for this project was a theory called 'Communicative Musicality'[1] which is the theory that the way we instinctively communicate to babies is inherently musical in nature. When an adult talks to a baby they will naturally use a sing-song voice, which you might know as 'baby talk'; psychologists call this Infant-Directed Speech (IDS), and there have been a number of studies in to the musical features of this type of communication.[2] The researchers have found that the way we talk to babies is very similar, both between different people, and even between different cultures. This is very interesting because if the musical speech patterns were caused by something in our environment (e.g. the type of music we are exposed to) then you would expect differences in cultures who use non-Western musical systems; however the musical features in IDS were remarkably similar regardless of culture, which suggests that these musical patterns are somehow innate, or hardwired in to our systems.

If we assume that this is true, that these patterns are instinctive to humans, then they must be important to our development of language, and communication and social skills. I started thinking about the children who haven't necessarily had access to this sort of input from their parents — perhaps they were neglected, or had unresponsive caregivers — and wondering whether it would be possible to take these musical patterns and features found in IDS, and embed them into other songs. Could this be beneficial for families like mine? As adopters we are taught that we need to 'fill in the gaps' in our child's development; could I do some of that with music?
As the project went on, I learnt more and more about how music affects us, and became more and more hooked on the subject. I learnt that when our fight/flight system activates, certain muscles in the middle ear shut down so we actually hear sounds differently,[3] and that

[1] Malloch, S., and Trevarthen, C. (eds) (2009), *Communicative Musicality: Exploring the basis of human companionship,* Oxford: Oxford University Press.

[2] Saint-Georges C., Chetouani M., Cassel R., Apicella F., Mahdhaoui A., Muratori F., et al. (2013) Motherese in Interaction: At the Cross-Road of Emotion and Cognition? (A Systematic Review). PLoS ONE 8(10): e78103.

[3] Porges, S. (2017), The Polyvagal Theory: The New Science of Safety and Trauma (talk). Retrieved from https://m.youtube.com/watch?v=br8-qebjlgs on 8 July 2019.

ADOPTING A MUSICAL APPROACH

Disney songs are great for keeping you calm! I became really interested in the autonomic nervous system, and how we can use music and movement to calm the nervous system down so that our cognitive functions can take over and manage our emotional state, and started to think about how we can connect with children when they are in a heightened state of anxiety, and begin to help their brains learn that they are safe, through interactive and musical play. I've tried to take what I've learned about some of the most basic, instinctive responses we have as humans, and think about how we can apply them consciously to our everyday lives to support our children's communication and social interactions, and ultimately, to help them feel safe.

In this book, I've tried to set out all the things I've learned in a way that's easy to digest. Each chapter relates to one song on the CD, in the order that they appear on the album. I've also 'themed' each chapter, so that you can flick through and get an idea of what each one is going to be about, and then hone in on the subject you need most right now. Every chapter has a communication theme, and a social/emotional theme, to reflect how you can use the songs in different ways for different purposes. For example, chapter 1 (What a funny sandwich) has a communication theme of turn-taking, and a social/emotional theme of agency and choice. Turn-taking is a key skill that underpins the ability to have a successful conversation, so I have built call and response sections into the song to let you practice this. I've also described how you can use the song to help your child practise making choices for themselves, and given a bit of background on why this might be difficult for them.

In each chapter there's a bit of background about the song, and the theory behind it, and then some suggestions of other games, songs, and activities relating to the chapter themes. I'm hoping this will be a book that you can dip in and out of as you need, the sort of thing that you might grab when you're thinking 'I really wish I had some fun ways I could encourage my children to take deep breaths' (chapter 11, for reference...). As always, you may have to adapt some of the songs and activities to suit your family — remember the ultimate goal is for this to be a fun, positive interaction where your child feels safe. If you think they are finding something tricky then stop straight away, and reassess, as it may be that you need to go in a bit more slowly, or build up their tolerance gradually. There are over 200 songs, games, activities, and resources referenced in this book, so I'm confident you will find something that suits you!

I've made a page on my website that will link you up to all the songs and resources I've mentioned in each chapter, so if there's a song you don't know, or a book you want to buy, you can go to catmcgill.uk/ AAMA-resources, scroll down to the appropriate chapter, and click through to the link you want.

I really hope you enjoy the songs, and I hope the book is helpful too. I always love to hear from people who have read my books so do look me up on social media — I'm @folkycat on Twitter, Facebook, Instagram, and YouTube.

Happy singing!

Cat x

'Adopting a Musical Approach' *was funded by Arts Council England, with support from the Folk Camps Society and an amazing team of Kickstarter backers.*

1
What a Funny Sandwich

Communication theme: turn-taking
Social/emotional theme: agency and choice

<u>Song lyrics</u>

I wake up on Monday morning, today I go to school
I like to wear my uniform, I think I'm looking cool
When it's time to go I'll put on my socks and shoes
But first mum is making sandwiches and now I have to choose

And she says...
Would you like ham?
Would you like cheese?
Or would you like a unicorn with knobbly knees?
What a funny sandwich that would be!

I wake up on Tuesday morning, it's football club today
We've got a big game coming up, I hope I get to play
I've found my football boots and socks and put them in my bag
But first dad is making sandwiches and asks me what I'll have

And he says...
Would you like jam?
Would you like spam?
Or would you like a panda with a frying pan?
What a funny sandwich that would be!

I wake up on Wednesday morning, I'm cycling today
I like the journey home best 'cos it's downhill all the way
My bag is packed, I've got my coat, I'll go and get my bike

CAT McGILL

But first Gran is making sandwiches and asks me what I'd like

And she says...
Would you like beef?
Or chocolate spread?
Or would you like a monkey with marshmallow on his head?
What a funny sandwich that would be!

I wake up on Thursday morning, it's my favourite day today
My best friend comes round after school and then we get to play
We chase each other round the park, go up and down the slide
But my brother's making sandwiches so first we have to decide

And he says...
Would you like crisps?
Or would you like egg?
Or would you like a tiger with a wooden leg?
What a funny sandwich that would be!

I wake up on Friday morning, it's cooking club at school
Sometimes we make pizza and sometimes strawberry fool
But I bet you'll never guess the recipe today?
That's right! We're making sandwiches! And now we all get to say

Oh...
Would you sweets?
Or a chocolate treat?
Or would you like an elephant with rabbit-sized feet?

Would you like cake?
Or raspberry mousse?
Or would you like a duck, a fish, a penguin, and a goose?
What a funny sandwich that would be!

Background

The ability to make choices about what happens to us is such a fundamental right that I imagine most people take it for granted, and simply don't think about it very often. However the power to make your own choice is something that is often denied to children, and especially children in the care system.

As adults we spend a lot of time telling children what to do, what to eat, what to say, and what to think — but how often do we let them practise making a choice for themselves? I know for myself as a parent that it's often so much easier and quicker to say 'this is what we're doing' than spend time explaining how to make the choice, or the reasoning behind the choice I've made. And of course, if your child has special needs or is non-speaking then they're likely to have even less say over the choices that are made for them on a day-to-day basis. Our education system trains children to do what they're told, and follow instructions — both important skills, obviously, but they must be balanced with teaching about choice, agency, and consent.

Children who are taken into care are at the extreme end of the scale regarding lack of choice and agency. They are taken away from their families and their homes (usually with little or no notice), and expected to continue living their life in a new house with strangers. They are allowed to see their parents if and when the local authority deems it appropriate; they might be moved on to a number of different foster homes, different schools, or back with their parents, all without having the opportunity to have any say over what happens to them. Some children who've experienced the care system react by trying to control everything around them, and some find it incredibly difficult to make any choice at all.

Now, this might all sound a bit heavy for a silly song about sandwiches, but if we are mindful of the underlying issue that we are trying to address, then this song has the potential to go from being a silly bit of fun to a useful tool for allowing children to learn about agency and practise making choices for themselves.

If we look in more detail at the make-up of the song, you'll notice that in the chorus section (where the sandwich choices are presented) there is always a gap after each type of sandwich, so that the children can shout out whether they like that type of sandwich. This encourages turn-taking, the first step to a call and response type dialogue (where one person says or sings something and someone else responds). This pattern of vocalising and waiting for a reply is an essential building block to communication and reciprocal interactions, as it's the skill that underpins conversation, and the ability to share an experience with another person. It's also a really important part of parent-child bonding, so once the song is familiar I'd encourage the parent to take the questioning role, and let the child respond. As the game is established, you can experiment with swapping roles and let the child do the asking — and see what type of sandwiches they come up with!

We can also take this to another level of detail and look at how some of the key features of Infant-Directed Speech (IDS) have been built in to the song. I'm still focusing on the chorus for this, as that is the part of the song where the parent-child interaction is taking place. (In this song the verses are just providing a bit of structure and a narrative around the chorus, which is the bit of the song that is most important in terms of opportunities for communication and development.)

Firstly, the melody shape at the start of the chorus where the pitch goes 'up-down-up-DOWN' (*'Would you like...'*) begins with the sinusoidal/bell curve that is often found in IDS when parents want to maintain a positive interaction[4]. As the tempo of the song has slowed, we are using the melody shape as another way of keeping the child's attention with the song.

Would you like ham?

(Sinusoidal means 'like a sine wave'. It's basically a gentle wave that goes up and down, like the shape you make when you wave a slinky. A bell curve is one of those 'humps', an upside-down U.)

---

[4] Saint-Georges C., Chetouani M., Cassel R., Apicella F., Mahdhaoui A., Muratori F., et al. (2013) Motherese in Interaction: At the Cross-Road of Emotion and Cognition? (A Systematic Review). PLoS ONE 8(10): e78103.

ADOPTING A MUSICAL APPROACH

The third question in each chorus (the silly one) plays on this even more by drawing out the sinusoidal contour even further: up-down-up-down-up-down-up-down-up-dooooowwwnnnn...

Would you like a un - i-corn with kno-bb-ly knees?

This drawn out melody shape further helps maintain the child's attention. I have also emphasised the falling contour at the end of each line (the melodic 'drop' at the end of the question, e.g. '*Would you like HAM?*', as in IDS a falling melodic contour is usually used with wh- questions. To help prepare you for all of that, the lead in to the chorus ('*And s/he says...*') uses a rising contour, which is often seen in infant-directed speech when a parent is trying to get the infant's attention or indicating to the infant that it's their turn to participate. Musically speaking, the rising contour is frequently used to build tension, or to indicate that there's something exciting about to happen.

Using the song

One of the biggest challenges of this project was to write these songs with a specific purpose, but make them fun and appealing to children so they want to listen to them over and over again, and don't realise that they are learning while they're doing it. When I wrote *What a funny sandwich*, I deliberately made it extremely silly, because I wanted children to get caught up in the fun of it, and use their imaginations, rather than worry about 'having' to make the choice.

The choice itself (within the song) is structured with clearly defined boundaries. You get three options; two are relatively sensible and one significantly less so. We've slowed down the tempo of the music in the chorus, and left a gap after each choice so that children have the option to respond if they want to.

Once the game is well established and the children are familiar with the song, and with the concept of responding to a choice of sandwich, you'll be able to take that chorus section and use it in a 'real life' situation when a choice needs to be made, giving the option for your children to respond. Don't be disheartened if this is difficult the first few times; go back to listening to the song and joining in together, and keep the focus on fun. The child may simply need more time to become familiar with the boundaries of the song so that they can understand and predict what will come next. Dan Hughes says that children who have suffered abuse and neglect often find it very difficult to join in (or even recognise) social interactions,[5] and often children will have difficulty with the process of having a conversation — the back and forth, call and response type interaction we have talked about. When you listen to the song with your child, make sure that you are modelling the response of yes or no (or however exuberant you want to be) to each sandwich type, and this will help your child to understand what is expected in the context of the song.

When you feel your child might be ready to try the song out in a real-life situation I'd recommend initially using it in exactly the same context, i.e. when you're making sandwiches. Remember this may be a novel way of interacting for your child, so they will need to be really familiar with it before they feel safe and confident enough to generalise it to other situations. Over time however, the song could easily be adapted to assist in any situation where choice is involved. You can change the words to suit the choice you want to make (e.g. would you like the park, or would you like home), and it absolutely doesn't have to rhyme, or scan, or fit in with the music — use it however you need it. If your child is familiar with the song, then using the melody they recognise will trigger the same emotions and reactions that they associate with the song (which is why it's really important to take it slow and focus on fun), which gives you a way of making new or difficult situations seem a little bit more familiar and safe.

---

[5] Hughes, D. (2017) 'Finding our way to reciprocity'. Ch 5 in Daniel, S., and Trevarthen, C. (eds.) *Rhythms of Relating in Children's Therapies*. London: Jessica Kingsley

ADOPTING A MUSICAL APPROACH

So, to summarise; you're absolutely welcome to just enjoy the song as a bit of silly fun to sing along to. However, if you'd like to give it a try for practicing choice-making or turn-taking conversation, this is what I'd recommend:

1) Listen to the song and sing along. Model responding to the sandwich choices. Talk about likes and dislikes. Make silly faces. Have fun!

2) Sing the chorus section with your child. Take turns being the one asking and the one responding, and have fun making up funny choices of sandwiches.

3) Use the chorus section in a real-life sandwich-making situation, and see if your child will respond to the choices you give them for an actual sandwich they're going to eat.

4) Use the chorus section in a non-sandwich related real-life situation, to offer your child a choice of two or three options.

If at any point you feel you've moved a bit too fast, or your child doesn't seem to cope with the next stage, just move back to the one before, and concentrate on the silly and fun elements in the song. Don't forget, underneath all of this your child is having to build trust and build a relationship with you, and it can take a lot of time and constancy before they really feel safe enough to play.

Managing choice in everyday life

If you've got a child who struggles to make choice — or if your child tries to control everything — it can be really beneficial to put some clear boundaries round the choice that needs to be made.

You can start really small, for example giving them a choice of which colour plate or bowl they have their dinner in. With Tickle, I would hold the bowls out in front of him, and he would touch the one he wanted. Some children might be able to verbalise the choice, others may only look at the one they want. It can be frustrating for us as parents if we really want our child to be able to speak to us, but we need to recognise that all of these ways are valid ways of making a choice, and accept the child at whatever level they are able to participate.

If your child can't or won't say their choice out loud, and you're not sure if they are looking at the object because they're choosing, or just because they're looking that way, then swap the objects over and ask them again — tell them you just want to make doubly sure, and can they please show you again which one they want. I can't imagine there are many children with enough self-control not to even sneak a quick look at the thing they want, though you may have to be watching closely to spot it!

If your child would find a face-to-face encounter like that too confrontational, then perhaps put the objects down within reach, and say that you're just going to pop over here and do something, but they should choose the thing they want and put it on the table. If you need to make it even less pressured, then say 'get' or 'bring' instead of choose.

Some children may find it easier to make choices by having the actual objects in front of them, others may like to choose based on pictures of objects, or symbols. You can make activity choice boards using photos or Makaton symbols, or a choice book with one activity on each page. If choice is a big issue for your child then you may have to take this really slowly, as it's really important that they feel safe before they are able to make the choice for themselves. For children who are not accustomed to having their needs met, be mindful that expressing a choice could make them feel very vulnerable.

ADOPTING A MUSICAL APPROACH

Games and activities to support choice making

I've added a selection of games and activities to support choice-making below. Remember these are supposed to be fun, low-pressure ways of practising the act of making a choice, within the safe boundaries of a game or activity. I've linked to songs and some of the more specific resources from my website catmcgill.uk/AAMA-resources.

Group games

Duck, duck, goose: Played in a seated circle, the person who is 'it' goes round tapping everyone on the head saying 'duck' each time; when they tap someone and say 'goose' the person who is goose has to chase them round the circle back to place, racing to sit in the empty space. Whoever is last is the new 'it', and gets to choose the next goose.

Cookie jar: Start up a rhythm of everyone clapping their knees and then their hands in time. Everyone chants the rhyme along to the rhythm:

All: *Who stole the cookie from the cookie jar?*
Leader: *[Picks a name] stole the cookie from the cookie jar*
Chosen child: *Who me?*
Everyone: *Yes you*
Chosen child: *Not I*
Everyone: *Then who?*
Chosen child: *[Picks a name] stole the cookie from the cookie jar*
 ... and carries on as above.

The game is to try and keep the rhythm going the whole time, and for each chosen child to pick up their line without missing a beat. I also remember playing this as a child with numbers, so each of us was given a number and we used those instead of names — it was extra tricky as you had to remember which number was you and respond in time!

CAT McGILL

Say your name: Everyone in the group takes it in turns to say their name in a funny voice (and with an action if you want!). Once a person has said their name, everyone has to copy their name in the same voice, and do the action.

Make a sound: In a circle, everyone chants '*Make a sound*' [two beats rest] '*Make a sound*' [two beats rest] and repeat. In the gaps each person takes it in turn to make a different sound with their voice or body. (NB a rest is a pause in the music with no sound.)

One-to-one games

Back pizzas: This is a Theraplay game using touch. Pretend to 'make' a pizza on the child's back, first spreading out the dough with smooth strokes, then ask the child to choose the 'toppings' they want. Tickle loves this game, and I use a different style of touch for each topping, and then pretend to eat him at the end! If your child doesn't enjoy touch then you could pretend together on a cushion, or using toy food.

Jenga/Kerplunk: As well as being exciting to play, games like Jenga and Kerplunk require the child to make a choice about which brick or straw they have to remove. I remember these games from my childhood, and there are loads of other games that use this same principle, so have some fun!

Musical activities

Musical activities provide ample opportunities for practising making choices, as well as enabling turn-taking interactions. The activities below can be done in group settings or one-to-one.

Choosing instruments: Have a selection of instruments in a bag or box, and let the child choose which one they want to play with. Encourage them to listen to the sound of each instrument to help them choose one they like. Warning: it will be noisy!

ADOPTING A MUSICAL APPROACH

Choosing songs: You can do this in a number of ways, the easiest of which is just to ask the child for a favourite song. Alternatively, you can use a choice board with symbols to represent each song, or have a bag with a variety of toys in, each one representing a different song, for example a toy cow for Old MacDonald.

Human jukebox: If your child is having difficulty making a choice in the activity above, then try taking a selection of symbols, cards, or toys that each represent a different song, and set them up on the floor in front of you. Whenever your child touches one of them, start singing the song for that item, and when they put it down, stop singing straight away. They will quickly pick up that it is their action triggering the starting and stopping of the song. Notice how they react to this — do they enjoy it? Do they keep going back to the same item, 'asking' you to start and stop? Let them lead the interaction completely, and watch carefully to see what happens.

Child-led music making: This can happen in a number of ways, in groups and one-to-one. Having an adult follow them in a musical activity is a very powerful thing for a child, and it can be a really good opportunity for bonding and building the relationship.

Improvisation: Have the child take the lead in how they want to play their instrument, and copy what they do. You might want to set up some choices (fast/slow or loud/quiet are the easiest ones to start with) or you can just let them play and join in with them. In a group you could take turns at letting a child lead.

Copycat: The most powerful way to do child-led music is to let the child play a rhythm or tune, and then when they pause, you copy *exactly* what they have just done as closely as you can, mimicking the speed and intensity of the playing. If you do this every time they pause, they will soon pick up on the game, and you may be able to have a really nice attuned back and forth interaction with them. I have used this activity many times in my work with non-verbal children in SEN schools, and have had teachers speechless with amazement at the interaction I've had from a child within one or two minutes.

Play and stop: Establish a signal for play, and a signal for stop — either a voice command, a noise, a hand movement, or some sort of symbol. The child indicates when it's time to play, and when it's time to stop, and everyone has to follow their lead. In groups, take it in turns to be the leader, but if you're one-to-one just follow the child's lead — this shows the child that you are completely focused on them.

Remember you don't have to have a house full of expensive musical instruments; a selection of pots and pans from your kitchen with some wooden spoons acting as drumsticks will do just fine!

<u>Songs</u>

Bungalow: There's a great campfire song (sometimes used as a warm up for choirs) called Bungalow, where each person takes it in turns to choose a dance move that everyone copies.

Boom chicka boom: I remember this song from the Girl Guides; it's mostly nonsense words, in a call and response style, done using different styles of voice. In the Guides we used to take turns at leading a verse using different voices. It is done in a rhythmic chant, rather than sung, so is a good one to do if you're not a confident singer. You could do this in a variety of ways: have the leader choose the next person along with the new style of voice, the new leader chooses the style of voice they want to do, or you could go round in a group and take it in turns to be the leader. If you're playing this in a big group, remember it's OK for a child to pass if they don't want to take the lead.

The farmer's in his den: (For younger children.) Played in a circle; a farmer is chosen to start and stands in the centre. Everyone sings the rhyme '*The farmer's in his den, the farmer's in his den, e-i-me-a-dee-o, the farmer's in his den*'. The farmer chooses a 'wife' to join them in the centre for the next verse (the farmer wants a wife), who them chooses a 'child' (the wife wants a child), who chooses a 'nurse' (the child wants a nurse), who chooses a 'dog' (the nurse wants a dog). Then everyone sings '*We all pat the dog*' together. (In some versions I've heard the dog wants a bone, and everyone ends up patting the bone.)

ADOPTING A MUSICAL APPROACH

The sandwich song: Another one! Although to be fair, this one predates mine. This is a fab song by the children's entertainer Keith Donnelly, where you can choose different sandwich fillings. I've linked to it from my resources page; Keith has loads of great songs for kids and it's also worth checking out his *Custard song*, which my daughter always found hilarious.

I am the music man: There's lots of versions of this song about choosing different musical instruments — you might also know it as Punchinello.

Everywhere we go: This is another great call and response song I remember from the Guides. In the version I've linked to from my website they just sing one verse, but we used to do loads of different ones: after the line '*and if they don't hear us*' the leader would say something like '*we'll speak a little louder*'/'*we'll speak a little quieter*'/'*we'll say it really posh*' etc.

CAT McGILL

2
Any finer thing

Communication theme: All about me
Social/emotional theme: Getting to know my body

Song lyrics

I've got a pair of clapping hands
Can you hear my hands go clap?
Have you ever seen any finer thing
Than a pair of clapping hands like that!

I've got a pair of stompy feet
Can you hear my feet go stomp?
Have you ever seen any finer thing
Than a pair of stompy feet like that!

I've got a pair of knocking knees
Can you hear my knees go knock?
Have you ever seen any finer thing
Than a pair of knocking knees like that!

I've got a very sniffy nose
Can you hear my nose go sniff?
Have you ever seen any finer thing
Than a very sniffy nose like that!

I've got a great big smiley mouth
Can you see my mouth go smile?
Have you ever seen any finer thing
Than a great big smiley mouth like that!

I've got a big round nodding head
Can you see my head go nod?
Have you ever seen any finer thing
Than a great big nodding head like that!

I've got a very jumpy body
Can you see my body jump?
Have you ever seen any finer thing
Than a very jumpy body like that!

I've got a pair of clapping hands
Can you hear my hands go clap?
Have you ever seen any finer thing
Than a pair of clapping hands like that!

Background

For this song I wanted to write an action song, involving different parts of the body, and this little idea just popped in to my head as I was getting ready for bed one night. I was remembering something that Fairy had said when she was about three, about having the stompiest feet, and could I hear her feet go stomp — and once I'd got that idea in my head the song just flowed from there!

When psychologists have studied Infant-Directed Speech (the way we talk to babies and young children), they've found some distinct characteristics in the melody of our words; even when we're not deliberately singing, our voice will still go up and down in pitch. One study found that adults tended to highlight new or important information in a sentence by putting it at the peak of the melodic contour,[6] or in other words, the highest pitch. (This is a similar idea to how we naturally raise the pitch at the end of a sentence when we're asking a question.) I've used this technique quite deliberately in this

---

[6] Papousek, M (1994), Melodies in caregivers' speech: A species specific guidance towards language, *Early Development and Parenting,* **3**, 5-17.

song, by having the first line of each verse getting higher in pitch, with the body part on the highest note. It's been really interesting seeing how Tickle responds to this song; he really enjoys it, and right from the start instinctively knew where the 'clap' should go in the song.

I've got a pair of clapp-ing hands

Interestingly, he also added in another clap/stomp/sniff at the end of each verse; I think he is tuning in to the falling melody of the final line ('...*than a pair of clapping hands like that*') which in IDS signals a finish, or the closing of a 'turn'.

than a pair of clapp-ing hands like that

In this final line, the melody falls back to the root note, which is what makes it sound 'finished'. This is a very common compositional technique used to signal the end of a musical phrase, and it's interesting how this mirrors the patterns found in IDS.

The communication and social/emotional themes for this song do overlap, as it's all about getting to know myself, and getting to know my body. This is an essential building block for safeguarding and consent; being able to name and talk about the different parts of my body, and understanding that my body belongs to me. You can't talk about your body or communicate a problem with a part of it unless you know how to think about it, and how to structure the language around the different parts of your body — and you can't do that until you know what each body part is and where to find it.

Some children will be further along than others in this aspect. You may need to start from a very sensory-focused, exploratory place if your child has trouble recognising the feelings in their body, or you might find you can go straight in at a language level. One of the most basic games you can play is simply to ask a child to point to a certain body part. This will give you a good idea of where they are at with their understanding of their body — start with easier things like hands and feet, and then move on to elbows, eyebrows, shoulders, ankles and so on. Remember we're always working on two levels with this; at one level we want to help our children experience their body, recognise the feelings and messages they are getting from it, and know how to use it, and on another level we want to make sure they have the language and cognitive understanding of their own body and bodily autonomy. These two things will go hand in hand — the word 'foot' is pretty meaningless unless you know what a foot is, where to find it, and what you're supposed to do with it.

Any finer thing is a fun action song, and who doesn't love clapping their hands and stomping their feet! Sing it together, join in with the actions, and even make up some new verses. You might also want to use this as an opportunity to have a discussion about public and private body parts, and why some body parts are not suitable for including in the song.

Everyday life

Children who have suffered from neglect in their early years may have missed out on some important opportunities for learning about their body. Have you ever noticed a baby frantically waving their arms and legs around when you talk to them? They are learning about their body and how they fit in to the world. Even just the normal everyday experiences like being carried around, changing direction, being rocked, and lying on their tummy instead of their back are huge learning experiences for babies as their bodily systems develop.[7]

---

[7] Lloyd, S. (2016), *Improving sensory processing in traumatized children,* London: Jessica Kingsley.

ADOPTING A MUSICAL APPROACH

If your child can't sit still, falls off chairs, bumps in to things, or has difficulty carrying a glass of water without spilling it then you might want to have a read of Sarah Lloyd's book, *Improving sensory processing in traumatized children*. (I've linked to it from my resources page on catmcgill.uk/AAMA-resources.) It's a great introduction to why some children find these things difficult, with practical suggestions to help. I've included various sensory activities throughout this book, but there are a few things you can incorporate in to your everyday life to help your child to fill in the gaps in their bodily systems.

Tummy time

When our children are babies we are all told how important tummy time is, but it's something you can also work on with older children. Let them watch TV whilst lying on their tummy propped up on their elbows, or maybe do some colouring or read a book together. When they've been doing this a while and have established more core strength, see if they can hold a 'Superman' pose, lying on their tummy with their arms and legs lifted off the floor.

Heavy work

Getting your child to carry heavy things can help with their proprioceptive sense (knowing where their body is). Pushing heavy objects will also help, if you have furniture that needs moving, or try exercises like wall push-ups or squats. Wall push-ups are just like normal push-ups except you do them against a wall instead of on the floor. For squats, have your back leaning against the wall and bend your knees until they're at a 90-degree angle, as if you're sitting on an invisible stool. It's very hard to maintain for a long period so you might want to practice building the time up slowly.

Rocking

Rocking motions are really good for helping children build bodily awareness. You can hold them to rock them if they're small enough, or encourage them to use rocking chairs, swings, or hammocks. We've just bought a hammock, and on the first day we tried it Tickle (who never stops moving) lay in it with me for nearly an hour, and asked to have his dinner in there. You could also get your child to lie on a blanket, then have two adults pick up the corners of the blanket and rock it like a makeshift hammock.

<u>Using the mouth</u>

Another great place for exploring body sensations is the mouth. Try things like popping candy, frozen grapes, crunchy crisps, and carrot sticks for exploring different textures. You could try taste testing, to see if your child can tell the difference between two flavours of crisps for example, or between jam and peanut butter, or a raspberry and a strawberry. Using an electric toothbrush can also be great for increasing stimulation in the mouth, or you could try drinking a really thick milkshake through a very small straw.

If you're concerned about your child's development you should always request an assessment from a qualified occupational therapist; however incorporating a few of these activities in to your daily life can be a great help in the meantime.

ADOPTING A MUSICAL APPROACH

<u>Games and activities for body awareness</u>

Below are a selection of games, songs, and activities that you can use to get to know your body a bit better. I've linked to the songs and some of the more specific resources from my website catmcgill.uk/AAMA-resources. There are also more body games in chapter 13 (Who), focused around connecting with and getting to know a child.

<u>Games</u>

Twister: A fantastic game for adults and children alike, this is perfect for practising rights and lefts, and building body strength as you try to balance. Newer versions of this game have options where you can choose a movement for the person who's turn it is, so you can really make it your own, and introduce some other body parts if you want to.

In a bind: This is a card game which I happened to support on Kickstarter a few years ago, and it's *brilliant*. You take it in turns to pick a card, and then you follow the instructions on that card, and keep following them until the end of the game. It might be things like sticking your tongue out, making a chicken noise every time you say something, having the card touching your arm at all times, having your elbow higher than your shoulder... you get the idea! As the game goes on everyone adds on a new action each round — but you have to keep doing the old ones. The first person to stop doing any one of their actions is out, and the game continues until there's only one person left. You can get all sorts of extensions to add new things to the game, and there's also a junior version for younger kids.

Pop the bubble: Blow a bubble and (if you can!) catch it on the bubble wand. Ask the child to pop the bubble with a particular body part, e.g. finger, ear, elbow etc. You could also blow a lot of bubbles and ask the child to pop them as quick as they can. This is quite a good way to do fun bubble play with a child who needs structure and boundaries to play well.

Balloon tennis: Try and keep a balloon in the air just using a specified body part.

Simon says: A classic children's game where one person gives instructions that everyone else has to follow — but only if the instruction is preceded by 'Simon says'. So if the instruction is 'Put your hands on your head' then you would do nothing, but if the instruction is 'Simon says put your hands on your head' then you would put your hands on your head.

Guess the body part: This could be a good game for car journeys if you get bored of I Spy; one person describes a body part (e.g. it's on your face in between your eyes and your mouth) and the others have to guess what it is.

Right or wrong: You make a statement about your (or your child's) body, and they have to tell you if you're right or wrong (e.g. I have six eyes). You can make it more fun, for example assigning a silly noise to wrong, or if you're playing with more than one child and have the space, assign a wall or chair in the room to be the 'right' station and the 'wrong' station, and the children have to run to the relevant point and touch it (or sit on it) depending on whether you're right or wrong.

Run and touch: The child has to touch different objects with a specified body part, e.g. touch a chair with your knee. If you have more than one child playing you can make it in to a race. You could level up the game by introducing numbers, e.g. touch six windows with your little finger.

<u>Songs for younger children</u>

There are so many of these that I could fill a whole book with them, but here are a few of my favourites. You will know a lot of them, I'm sure.

Head, shoulders, knees and toes: The classic! Don't forget that you can extend the main song by repeating it but just doing the action without the word — the first time just leave a gap for 'head' but sing the rest, the next time leave a gap for 'head' and for 'shoulders', and so on, taking out one word each time. Once you've done it through with no words at all, only actions, then you can do a final time singing the whole thing through as loud as you can.

Have you ever seen a penguin come to tea: This song is brilliant fun, and you get to play at being penguins! As the song builds up you add another body part in to the dance each time.

Hokey cokey: Another classic, great to play in a big circle. You can adapt this for whichever body parts you want — shoulders, elbow, knees etc.

There's a spider on the floor: In this song the spider climbs up on to various different body parts. It would be good fun to do with a toy, or a tickly-finger-spider that crawls over the body parts when they come up in the song.

One finger, one thumb, keep moving: I don't know how much this song is sung these days but it was a staple of my childhood. It's another cumulative song that adds extra body parts each time through.

Nicky nacky nocky noo: This is another one of those songs that I can't even remember where I first heard it, but it seems to have been around forever. It's a cumulative body part song, using silly words for the different parts of the body.

Songs for older children

Hi, my name's Joe: This is a more grown up version of the cumulative body part songs above, a song that gets you to move different parts of your body, adding a new one each time. It's done as a chant or a rap rather than sung.

I'm being eaten by a boa constrictor: This was originally written by Shel Silverstein, but the version I found of him singing it online is so different to the one I know I think it's suffered from the Chinese

Whispers effect. It was written to be sung continuously, but you could also do it cumulatively by repeating the '*I'm being eaten*' section and add on a new body part each time.

Baby 1, 2, 3: I've added this in the 'older children' section because I first learnt it as a clapping game, but you can just as easily use it for younger children. The version I've linked to is quite short, you can add more body parts and do it however long you like. It's essentially a more mature version of *Head, shoulders, knees and toes.*

Musical activities

Exploring instruments: One of my favourite things to do with children is just give them a musical instrument and let them explore it. It doesn't have to be expensive — you can often find old guitars or accordions in charity shops. I like to encourage children to see what different noises they can make from the instrument, and to feel how the instrument vibrates when they play it. (Sensory-seeking children will love this.) You could experiment with putting the instrument on to different parts of their body to play it — for example have a child lie on the floor and rest the body of the guitar on their tummy, and see if they can feel the vibrations when you strum it. This activity will help children focus in on different parts of their body and what they can feel there. You can do this with any instrument, as there will always be an element of vibration, though stringed and percussion instruments are best for really feeling it in the body of the instrument.

Body percussion: Body percussion refers to any noise that is made by the body — clapping your hands, stamping your feet, clicking your fingers, and so on. You can do very simple riffs (for example, 'stamp stamp clap' will give you the riff from *We will rock you*) or you can build up and make them as complicated as you like. Your child might enjoy looking at videos of the percussive theatre group Stomp, who build up incredible performances with layered patterns of sound. Or, if you want something a little bit different, try looking up the videos of South African gumboot dancing that I've linked from my resources page.

3
Little fish's Big Journey

Communication theme: Telling a story
Social/emotional theme: Life story/loss

<u>Song lyrics</u>

It was early one morning when the sun began to rise
The rabbits and the foxes rubbed the sleep out of their eyes
The trees along the riverbank were rustling their leaves
And a newborn baby caterpillar woke up with a sneeze

Down beneath the surface on the stony riverbed
A little fish was stirring, gave a yawn and rubbed his head
He looked around with sleepy eyes and gave a little quiver
And nervously he whispered 'I don't think I know this river'

'It looks a bit like my river, but that's a different stone
And those weeds growing in a clump are usually alone
The water is much clearer here, a lovely sparkling blue
But though it's nice, it's not my home! I don't know what to do!'

As he sadly gazed around, the fish began to cry
'I don't know how I got here, and I've no idea why
I'm frightened, but I'm angry! And I've had enough of crying!'
He crossly flicked his tail and sent a waterboatman flying

A wise old frog sat on a rock had watched the scene unfold
She reached for fish's flailing fin and gently took a hold
'Last night a heavy rainstorm made the river overflow
It swept you down and let you here, it's quite a shock, I know.'

CAT McGILL

The fish looked up quite startled, but his memory was stirring
And he suddenly had flashbacks of the tumbling, the whirling
The frog hopped down to sit with him and said 'It's fine to cry'
'Those feelings that were stuck inside, it's time to let them fly'

'Sometimes in life you see the changes coming round the bend
And other times they shock you with a start, a move, an end
Sometimes they'll make you angry, sometimes they'll make you sad
Sometimes you might feel nothing, and sometimes you'll be glad'

'One thing you must remember' went on the wise old frog
'If ever you feel lonely, you're welcome at my log
It's bound to take a while to get used to your new home
But I will always be here, you'll never be alone'

As time went on the little fish grew happier again
Though he always would think fondly of his home lost to the rain
And if you're looking closely one day near the river bend
You just might see a little fish, and his wise old froggy friend

Background

Loss is such a massive part of our children's lives that I knew I had to somehow capture that in one of the songs. I thought long and hard about the best way to do it, how to make sure I faced up to the issue and the huge feelings involved, whilst still writing a song that children could also enjoy listening to and singing along to.

I decided in the end to make it in to a story. I'd already had the idea of using a river metaphor, where I could use the idea that the water essentially stays the same as it moves down the river, but is somehow slightly different as well (this later turned in to *The River*, chapter 14), but I knew I needed to go a bit more literal, so introduced the idea of a fish who gets swept down the river in a storm.

ADOPTING A MUSICAL APPROACH

The story starts with the fish waking up in an unfamiliar place, not quite knowing what's happened. It was quite important to me to start the story this way, as I think it reflects the experience of so many of our children when they're taken in to care — even if not literally waking up in a new place (though that is possible in some cases), that sense of having been swept along in something you don't understand, and having to work out retrospectively what on earth has happened to you.

In the song the fish goes through a range of emotions. I deliberately didn't offer him any suggestions for dealing with them; I wanted to state them, and accept them for what they are without trying to change or excuse them. We're dealing with big, big feelings here, and the first step is always learning to sit with them, even when they're uncomfortable.

Fish is supported in the song by his new friend the wise old frog, who encourages him to reflect on what he's feeling, and remember that he can ask for help when he needs it. It was really tempting to give them a big uplifting 'happy ever after' kind of finish, but that wouldn't have been at all realistic. Instead I've tried to capture the mix of feelings — yes, life goes on, and it's possible to be happy, but you don't forget what has gone before.

In terms of the songwriting, the lyrics and the storytelling were my main focus, so those were what I wrote first. The melody in this case simply acts as a vehicle for telling the story, so I've kept it quite simple, and used a gentle rising and falling melody to emulate the water flowing along the river.

Storytelling and traumatic memories

The ability to tell a story might seem fairly trivial, but cognitively it's a complex process involving memory and understanding, and it's a particularly important skill for children who have experienced trauma. When a child experiences a traumatic event such as abuse, neglect, or being removed from their family, the memory of that event will be stored in their body in a different way to other, non-traumatic memories.[8] Traumatic memories are often fragmented, without context, and they're not time-tagged, meaning they are experienced as if they're happening *right now*. The child doesn't so much *think* about the memory, as *feel* like it's happening to them all over again. This can be especially difficult if the child didn't really understand what was happening to them at the time.

I've written about memory in my first book *Me, the Boy, and The Monster*, so I won't go in to it in great detail here, but in summary, different experiences are stored differently in the body and in the mind; a memory of what you had for dinner last night is stored differently to the memory of how to ride a bike, for example. If you want to talk to someone about something that has happened to you (let's say, what you had for dinner last night), you have gone through a series of steps to be able to get to that point:

- You've got a cognitive understanding of the event that happened. (I was hungry, I had dinner.)

- Your brain has stored that understanding as a memory. (You can recall details of the event such as what you had to eat.)

- You are able to retrieve that memory as and when you want to. (If someone asks you can tell them, but you don't dwell on it all day or find it coming back to you suddenly.)

- You are able to relate the memory to someone else, as a 'story'.

When you consider what happens after a traumatic event, the process will be somewhat different:

- You may not remember exactly what happened. (You might have a mix of feelings and flashbacks.)

---

[8] Brewin, C.R., Dalgleish, R., and Joseph, S. (1996), 'A dual representation theory of post traumatic stress disorder', *Psychological Review 117(1)*, 210–232.

ADOPTING A MUSICAL APPROACH

- You don't really know what happened, but your body will remember
  the feelings.
(You might not be able to find the words to describe what happened,
but will experience the feelings as if you were back there experiencing
it again.)

- You might experience unwanted triggers that bring the memory and
  feelings back to the fore
(Experienced as unexpected and intrusive flashbacks, rather than
because you're trying to remember what happened.)

- You find it difficult to explain to someone else what has happened,
because it feels to raw, or it's too traumatic to 'relive' the experience

As you begin to process what has happened to you, you will naturally
start to make sense of it and become more able to tell the story of
what happened. In terms of your brain, this now means that memory
can be stored with other long term memories and can be recalled
safely without feeling like you've regressed back to when it happened.
One of the aims of talking therapy is to help you create these stories
about things that have happened to you, so that they can be processed
and stored in your brain in a way that means they have much less
impact on your daily life.

So, circling back round to storytelling again; before a child can begin
to process a traumatic experience, they have to be able to think about
it as a 'story' of something that happened to them, rather than
experiencing the memory as if it was happening right now. This in
itself can be a traumatic and drawn-out process, and often is best
managed with a qualified therapist. However, as you may have
experienced, children live with their trauma twenty-four hours a day,
which means there is a significant amount of processing that has to
happen outside of the therapy room. In our case, Tickle's therapist
ended up being more of a support to Husband and myself as we dealt
with Tickle's disclosures and behaviour in day-to-day life. This is a
long, long process, and don't be surprised if your child needs to repeat
the same things over and over for weeks or months on end.
Understanding that Tickle needed to be able to make things into a

story really helped me to support him, and there was one point where we would have long conversations at bedtime every day for months, going over the same questions again and again as he pieced things together in his mind.

Using the song

I wrote *Little fish's Big Journey* to use as a prompt for conversations about life stories, and the emotions around them. You don't have to do this every time you listen to it, or at all in fact — all of the songs on the album can be enjoyed in their own right — but if it's something you think would be useful, then using the song as a starting point might be an easier way in to the topic. It's important that you go slowly and let the child lead, as they really need to feel safe in order to talk about these difficult feelings.

The first thing to do would be to ask the child what they think the song is about, or see if they can tell you the story of the song as they've understood it. Are they able to interpret the story correctly? Can they tell you how the fish is feeling at the beginning of the story? The middle? The end? Are they able to say what has caused the fish to feel that way?

I would recommend keeping this really light touch; you want to aim for a casual chat rather than an inquisition; just think of how you might approach it if this were a story book you were reading together. Tickle will often pick up on a word or phrase as we're listening to the song, and that can be an opening to a conversation. (Listening to the album in the car might be beneficial, as children often find difficult conversations easier to manage when there is no expectation of face-to-face contact.)

If your child can tell the story of the fish, can they relate it to any of their own experiences? When you're talking to them about it, it can be useful to use the words that your child has used to describe the story, as this will help affirm you are really listening to them. Ask them whether they know how the fish feels, and whether anything has ever happened to them that's made them feel like that?

ADOPTING A MUSICAL APPROACH

It might be interesting to talk about the end of the song. What do they think happened after the song finished? How does the fish feel now? Do you think he will stay friends with the frog?

You could also ask your child how they would describe the frog in the song. Can they think of a time in their life when someone has been kind to them, like the frog is kind to the fish? Or when they have been kind to someone else?

Don't worry if your child talks about school, or friendships, or their toys, when you are really hoping they might talk about their trauma, and definitely don't try and force the issue. They will come to it when they are ready, and in the meantime you are laying down strong foundations for them to be able to talk about it, and giving them the tools to do so. Every time your child tells a story, or talks about feelings, they are practising the skills they will need to be able to process and understand their own life story.

Everyday life

In your everyday life, there is no one 'right' way to approach life story work. Some people have life story books made by a social worker, other people make their own, or make photo albums, story books, or whatever they feel is suitable for their child. The important thing to remember is that it's not something you do once and then put it on the shelf. Your child will need to ask a lot of questions, probably the same ones over and over; they will need to talk through things again and again, look at their book again and again. I've found that topics cycle back round at certain times of year, and things that we've been over and understood on one level get revisited again at a deeper level the next time round.

You will already know that life story work isn't something that just 'happens' at a designated time; there may be any number of opportunities throughout your normal day to help your child make sense of their past, and it's important they know that you are open to discussing it. I asked my friends on Adoption Twitter for their best tips for life story activities, and suggestions ranged from a colour coded timeline of all the people and places their child had lived with or in, to a photo album that you could keep adding to, which includes birth and foster families to show that it's all part of one life and not separate pieces. One artistic adopter had created a comic book for her child, to tell his life story in a way that really appealed to him.

Something that our therapist encouraged us to do was help Tickle gain an experiential understanding of what 'good' parenting looks like, so he could have a reference point for understanding some of the things he has missed out on, and — crucially — begin to realise that it wasn't his fault that he didn't get them. Tickle was fascinated with baby photos of Fairy (who is my birth child) and used to spend hours looking at them and asking questions about when she was a baby. This coincided with a phase where he would frequently regress and pretend to be a baby himself, so I would say to him 'Would you like me to show you how I would have looked after you if I'd known you when you were a baby?' If he was amenable (which he always was) then I could say 'I would have cuddled you like this, and given you a drink like this...' while doing it with him. This was a lovely bonding experience for us, and helped to reinforce for him that the things that happened to him *weren't* normal, and weren't caused by anything that *he* did wrong. We had to explicitly teach him that this is how adults are *supposed* to look after children, and it is not your fault that this didn't happen for you.

The child's understanding of adoption

Research that was done in the early 1980s identified some distinct stages children go through in their understanding of adoption[9], and although the ages given below are approximate and will vary for each child, it might be useful to bear in mind your child's level of understanding when you are attempting life story work with them.

---

[9] Brodzinsky, D. M., Singer, L. M., and Braff, A. M. (1984), 'Children's understanding of adoption', *Child Development, 55*(3), 869-878.

ADOPTING A MUSICAL APPROACH

1. Approximate age 0–4 years. Children exhibit no understanding of adoption. However, children learn to like and dislike things that their parents like and dislike, so during this stage parents can focus on using the word 'adoption' in a positive and relaxed way, so the child learns to be comfortable talking about it.

2. Approximate age 4–6 years. Children know the words 'adoption' and 'birth' but don't really understand what they mean or the difference between them. They might believe that all children have to leave their birth parents and are given a new family. It could be beneficial to help children develop a simple story to use when talking to their friends at school or nursery.

3. Approximate age 6–8 years. Children can differentiate between adoption and birth as different ways of entering a family. They accept what their parents and social workers have told them about adoption being permanent, but don't really understand why. They can understand simple reasons why their birth parents could not keep them.

4. Approximate age 8–10 years. Children differentiate between adoption and birth, but may now have some insecurities about the permanence of the adoptive relationship. The child's thought processes are now more complex, which means they can have a more sophisticated understanding of what has happened to them, rather than taking what parents and professionals have said at face value. This can lead to some anxiety and doubt, and the child may begin to really grieve for what they have lost. They might also worry that their adoptive family may have to give them up if their circumstances change, for example if a parent loses a job.

5. Approximate age 10–12 years. The child moves on to more abstract levels of thought, and can understand things at a deeper, more adult level. Their identity is bound up in being related to two families, and they need to understand their place in each one. Contact with their birth family can be really important to help with this.

As you can see, each stage builds upon the last, so it is beneficial to be honest with a child (at an age-appropriate level) right from the start so they can build their understanding of adoption and how this feeds in to their self-concept. (Chapter 5 (Me) has more activities around building a positive self-concept in children.)

ADOPTING A MUSICAL APPROACH

Resources and activities for supporting life story work

'Games' didn't really seem like an appropriate title for this section, so instead I've listed some useful resources that you might want to look at if you want more information about how to approach life story work, and suggested a few activities. I have linked to all of the resources from my website catmcgill.uk/AAMA-resources.

Useful websites: There's a really good summary page at firststeps.first4adoption.org.uk/exercises/life-story-work which explains why life story work is important, and gives an overview of how to create a life story book. The website www.lifestoryworks.org/ has step-by-step guides to creating a life story book.

Useful books: Joy Rees is one of the long-time experts in life story work, and her book *Life story books for adopted and fostered children* is available from Jessica Kingsley Publishers. It explains the theory and reasoning behind life story books, as well as how to structure them, and gives five different examples of life stories for five fictional children in different situations. Joy also has a lot of resources on her website: thejoyoflifework.com.

Kim Golding's book *Using Stories to Build Bridges with Traumatized Children* is a really excellent resource if you want to explore your child's past using stories. Kim shows you how to build and create stories that serve different purposes, and the book comes with twenty-one stories, all categorised and themed, with suggested age ranges.

One of the original books exploring life story work was Vera Fahlbeg's *A Child's Journey Through Placement*. Fahlberg first developed the concept of the parent game that I've described below.

You might also like to try *Life Story Work with Children who are Fostered or Adopted: Creative Ideas and Activities* by Katie Wrench and Lesley Naylor. This is a practical book with a lot of tried and tested activities that are suitable for children at different stages of their understanding.

Useful videos: On my website resources page I have linked to a video of a talk by Helen Oakwater which describes how important it is to tell age-appropriate truths to adopted children, so that the narrative they are given matches their sensory memories.

Special Stories **app**: This is an app that lets you create social stories on an iPad or tablet, with photos, text, and voice recordings. You can either read the stories within the app (in which case it will play the voice recording of each page) or you can export to a pdf or to iBooks.

Project Life: These are scrapbook type resources which you can use to build a flexible and easily adapted life story book. Adoption blogger Hannah Meadows has given an extensive review of the Project Life resources on her website, linked from my resources page.

Bedtime stories: One of the things I frequently do with Tickle is tell him the story of our day at bedtime. I tell it in the third person, as if I were telling a fairytale: 'Once upon a time there was Mummy and Dad and Tickle, and one day they woke up really early and had some yummy Weetabix for breakfast…' I go through the whole day as a story, and Tickle adds in any bits I've forgotten. He's totally engaged in the process, much more so than when I read him a book at bedtime, where he's likely to fidget or chat. I'm hoping that this will give him some good foundations for finding the words to tell his own story.

A bag of feelings: You can do this activity with a drawing of a bag, or an actual bag. The idea is to help your child talk about their feelings, so you start by saying to your child 'If this was a bag of all the feelings inside you, I wonder what would be in there?' Your child can write or draw them on a piece of paper to put in to the bag, or choose a different colour piece of paper (or ball) for each different feeling, to show you how many of each are in the bag. Be curious, and ask gentle questions to see if you can uncover more information about the feelings, like 'I wonder which of the feelings get bigger when we talk about your birth family?'. Try to end the activity on a positive note, and maybe put some hopes, dreams, or fun memories in to the bag as well.

ADOPTING A MUSICAL APPROACH

Memory jar: This activity can be used to help children who want to keep memories of significant people, and can help structure a safe way of thinking about them. You can create the jar in any way you like, for example painted stones, buttons, or sand. If you use different colours of sand you can explain that each one can represent a different memory, and even though the colours might get mixed up, they are all still in there. Some children might want to be able to take out the stones or buttons to hold them and think about the memories, or others might like to write a memory down on a piece of paper.

The parent game: The idea of this game is to help children understand some of the different aspects of being a parent, and start to think about why they may have been separated from their birth family. You need a list of things that parents do for children under three headings: hereditary things (some versions of this activity use 'born to' as an easier label for a child to understand), parenting things, and legal (or decision) things. Examples of hereditary things could be how tall we are, what colour our eyes or hair are, what illnesses we might get, our talents, personality, etc. Parenting things could be keeping us warm, making sure we have enough food, taking us to the dentist, making sure we are clean and have toys and books, taking us to school on time, and so on. Legal things could include permission to go on school trips, to have an operation, choosing which school we go to, giving permission to go on sleepovers, choosing our name and registering our birth. You can cut these up and put them in boxes or bags, or just look at them on a list. Encourage your child to think about all the different things that go in to parenting, and how difficult it might be to do all of them if you have difficulties of your own. Explain that parents have to do *all* of those things, all of the time, until the child is grown up and can look after themselves. From this point you can adapt the activity to whatever is suitable for your child; perhaps you could put all the items in to a big bag and jumble them up, then take them out one at a time and sort them again, or you could talk about your child's favourite TV or book characters and pick out examples of how their parents do those things for them.

CAT McGILL

4
Hide and seek

Communication theme: Play
Social/emotional theme: Attachment

<u>Song lyrics</u>

Someone's hiding, someone's seeking
I wonder where you could be?
Someone's watching, someone's creeping
Are you going to jump out on me?

And I can't wait to see your face
When I find you in your hiding place
Are you excited too?
So now what shall we do?

Shall we...
Jump on the bed and scream?
Pretend it's a trampoline?
Shall we paint our faces green?
Now I've found you
Shall we go and fly a kite?
Do a headstand on your bike?
We can do anything we like!
Now I've found you

Now I've found you, now I've found you
We can do anything we like now I've found you

Someone's hiding, someone's seeking
I wonder where I'll find you?

CAT McGILL

Someone's watching, someone's creeping
I'll keep looking 'til I do

And I can't wait to see your face
When I find you in your hiding place
Are you excited too?
And now what shall we do?

Shall we...
Dive in to a cake?
Or a melted chocolate lake?
Shall we slither round like snakes?
Now I've found you
Shall we hunt for secret clues?
Buy a pair of purple shoes?
We can do anything we choose
Now I've found you

Now I've found you, now I've found you
We can do anything we like now I've found you
Now I've found you, now I've found you
We can do anything we like now I've found you

And now what shall we do?

Take a tiger to the park?
Teach an elephant to bark?
Go swimming with a shark?
Now I've found you
Shall we squash a hundred peas?
Build a castle out of cheese?
We can do anything we please
Now I've found you

Now I've found you, now I've found you
We can do anything we like now I've found you
Now I've found you, now I've found you
We can do anything we like now I've found you

ADOPTING A MUSICAL APPROACH

<u>Background</u>

Hide and seek is such an important game for children who have been removed from their families. It allows them to experience the feelings of loss and separation from a caregiver *in a safe and contained way*, with the feelings quickly resolved when they are 'found'. This pattern of repeatedly raising and then reducing anxiety in the child (through play) helps build their ability to predict positive interactions, and to trust their caregivers.[10] Or, to put it more simply, the child begins to believe that you care about them enough to come and find them.

You might have noticed that although this song is about hiding, the main focus of the lyrics is on fun things we can do '*now I've found you*'. This was a deliberate decision; the finding (and the belief that you are going to be found) is the most important part of the game, so I wanted to make that the most important part of the song. If you think about it in terms of the pattern of raised and lowered anxiety, the hiding raises the anxiety, and the finding lowers it — so this song is designed to reinforce that positive state of being found. I added in lots of silly suggestions of things we could do '*now I've found you*' to reinforce the fun, positive emotions with humour. What we're trying to do is build the child's sense of trust in you, as their caregiver, to meet their needs consistently. In other words, we're trying to support your child in forming a secure attachment to you.

Attachment is something we hear a lot about as adoptive parents. It's a word that psychologists use to describe the relationship that a child has to their caregivers, but it's one that's often misunderstood and misappropriated in the context of adoption. I believe adoption professionals often place too much focus on simply building an attachment relationship, believing that's what is needed in order for the child to be settled and secure. They're not wrong as such; attachment is really important, but with a traumatised adopted child it's not the end goal, it's the *start* of the healing process. In order to

---

10 Hasler, J. (2017), 'Healing Rhythms: Music Therapy for Attachment and Trauma', in Hendry, A. and Hasler, J. (2017), *Creative Therapies for Complex Trauma,* ch. 7, pp 135–153. London: Jessica Kingsley.

fully understand this it's helpful to take a brief look at what we actually mean by attachment.

When a child has a secure attachment to an adult, they feel safe. They are confident that, whatever happens, the adult will be available to meet their needs. They can take comfort from their caregiver when they're upset, and their caregiver can help them to regulate their emotions and calm down. The child can try new things, explore their environment, because they know that the caregiver will be there when they need to return to them. When faced with new situations the child relies on the caregiver as a 'safe base' from which they can explore and experiment. They can be brave, because they feel safe enough to make themselves vulnerable.

Attachment is important because all a child's learning, all their healing, all their positive emotional growth can only develop from a place of feeling safe and secure, *and that feeling of safety comes from the attachment relationship*. It's not just about being physically safe, being warm and fed, but being able to trust that someone else is going to consistently provide that for you. The game of hide and seek allows the child to test this out within the context of a game — are you going to keep looking for them? Do you care enough about them to try and find them?

Circling back round to the song, what I have tried to do is keep the focus almost entirely on the feeling of safety, of being 'found', and exploring all the new and exciting things we could do together. I've deliberately made the melody rise quite steeply at the start of that section ('*Jump on the bed and scream...*') as this melody shape is used in Infant-Directed Speech (IDS) to grab attention. The chorus section ('*Now I've found you...*') is made up of repeated falling lines of melody, which are used in IDS for relaxing and soothing — now I've found you, you're safe, you can relax.

Using the song

The idea behind the verse ('*Someone's hiding...*') is that once the child is familiar with the song, these lines could be taken out as a discrete section and used in a game of hide and seek. If you want to do this you can change the word 'someone' to the name of whoever is playing the game, so in my case I would sing 'Tickle's hiding, Mummy's seeking'. The melody I've used for this line follows a sinusoidal (up and down) contour which is used in IDS to hold attention. It's great for creating anticipation and drawing you in to the song, so you could make it part of the game to sing that line really slowly to draw out the build-up while you're looking for the child.

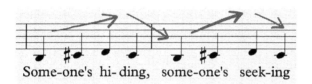

Some-one's hi-ding, some-one's seek-ing

Singing or chanting something while you are looking for your child will help keep a connection with them even though they may not be able to see you, and will help reassure them that you are keeping them in mind, and that you are still looking for them. This will help build the idea of 'permanence'; that something (or someone) continues to exist even when you can't see them, and will help them to tolerate being separated from you. (There's more about permanence in chapter 12 (Chat away).)

To finish the game, use the reassuring '*Now I've found you*' chorus section to reinforce the positive feelings when you are reunited with the child.

Nurturing attachments in everyday life

As with anything, there is no one 'right' way to approach attachment building with your child, but the key is always going to be consistency. Be aware that your child will test you, they will push and push against you because they need to know whether there is a point where you will decide you've had enough and give up on them. When children have experienced loss of an attachment figure (or more than one, if they have had multiple moves) they can understandably find it difficult to trust that it isn't going to happen again, and consequently will not want to make themselves vulnerable by relying on someone they believe is also going to leave them. Much as we may not want to admit it, the very process of removing a child from their caregiver creates additional trauma on top of what they may have experienced with their birth family, regardless of whether or not it was the 'right' thing to do.

Don't underestimate how confusing it can be for children as they try to work out who is who in their new family. You may have heard of 'funnelling' or have been advised to do it by a social worker; it refers to the idea that when you first adopt a child, you are the one who fulfils all their needs, in order to 'teach' them that you are now their caregiver. So if we're out with Gran and Tickle wants a drink, the theory is that Husband or I should be the ones to get it for him, so he understands that we are the ones who now look after him. I have mixed feelings about funnelling — on one hand it can leave new adoptive parents very isolated in the early days, but on the other hand I've seen how confusing it has been for Tickle as he's tried to work out who he can rely on to meet his needs. It took him quite a while to accept that my daughter wasn't another adult who could look after him (she was eight when he moved in), as he couldn't understand the difference between Fairy being able to get him a drink (which she was happy to help with) and being able to drive him to his swimming lesson (which was somewhat more problematic). If this sort of thing is something that your child struggles with, you might want to consider funnelling for a while to see if that helps. As I write this, Tickle has been living with us for nearly four years, and even now he needs to check in regularly with me that I'm still his mummy; it's important that I continue to take that question seriously, no matter how many times I've answered it.

The good news is that even if a child hasn't had a secure attachment relationship in the past, it is still perfectly possible for them to have one within subsequent relationships.[11] It's been interesting (and quite an experience) to watch how Tickle goes about making attachment

---

[11] Siegel, D., and Sroufe, A. (2011), *The Verdict is In,* retrieved from https://www.drdansiegel.com/uploads/1271-the-verdict-is-in.pdf on 9 June 2019.

relationships with adults. What we've noticed is that he has gone through a phase with each of the important adults in his life where he really tested us, to see whether we would stick. He did this one adult at a time — first everything was directed at me (violence, aggression, shouting etc), then all of a sudden it wasn't any more, and it was Husband who would bear the brunt of it. Then, to a lesser extent, Gran had a bit of a test, and most recently Tickle's favourite teacher at school, and one of the teaching assistants. If you don't realise what's driving the behaviour it can be incredibly upsetting, and Husband and I had to really reassure Tickle's poor teacher that he wasn't hitting her because he didn't like her, but because he loves her and needs to know that she's not going to leave him. This won't necessarily be the same for every child, but if you've noticed a similar pattern it might be worth thinking about what's behind it.

The thing about human relationships is that we all bring our own baggage to them, and it's sometimes helpful to be aware of how our child's behaviour might be triggering something within ourselves that isn't entirely about the child in front of us. Having said that, you absolutely don't need to be perfect, and modelling how to make a mistake in a relationship and apologise for it is a valuable lesson, and a completely normal part of social interaction. Research has shown that the best predictor for a child having a secure attachment is actually *not* how well the parent is attuned to the child's needs, but how well they can 'repair' the relationship when there is a mismatch or a falling out,[12] and that even where there is a secure attachment present, the adult is only actually tuned in to the child's needs about 30 per cent of the time.[13] This is great news for us as parents, as we often put a lot of pressure on ourselves to be perfectly attuned to our child, and meeting their needs 100 per cent of the time, when it's really not necessary. Additionally, research in to adult attachment suggests that having a secure attachment relationship in childhood is not as important as how

---

[12] Tucker, J. (2018), 'Panksepp and Biven's 7 primary process emotional systems, and how they inform our understanding and practice'. Presentation as part of a course run by OXPIP, 22 January 2018.

[13] Tronick, E. Z., and Gianino, A. (1986), 'Interactive mismatch and repair: Challenges to the coping infant', *Zero to Three, 6*(3), 1–6.

well you have dealt with anything that has happened to you; how well you've understood it, and how you've constructed the narrative of your own life story.[14] Attachment is really important, but we do need to remember it's part of a bigger picture.

---

[14] Main, M., Kaplan, N., and Cassidy, J. (1985), 'Security in Infancy, Childhood, and Adulthood: A Move to the Level of Representation', *Monographs of the Society for Research in Child Development*. Vol. 50, No. 1/2, Growing Points of Attachment Theory and Research, pp. 66–104.

ADOPTING A MUSICAL APPROACH

<u>Games and activities to support attachment</u>

Remember, an attachment is simply a description of the relationship between a child and a caregiver, so you don't need to worry about 'making' an attachment, it will happen very naturally. However what you can influence is the quality of that attachment, so these activities are designed to help build up the positive interactions between you and your child.

I've got three chapters dedicated to attachment and relationship building in this book, so I've taken a slightly different slant on the games and activities section in each. This chapter focuses on playful, fun games that are great for bonding and will allow you to sneak in a bit of nurture for children who find that hard. Chapter 10 (I will love you) has lots of face-to-face games for children who can manage a more intense interaction, and chapter 13 (Who) focuses on nurture games that involve the whole body.

All the songs I've listed below are linked from catmcgill.uk/AAMA-resources as an easy reference guide.

Peekaboo: This beloved game of babies and toddlers actually has real cognitive value, helping children to develop the idea that objects and people exist even when you can't see them. Psychologists call this 'object permanence'. (There are more permanence and separation games and activities in chapter 12 to go with the song *Chat away*.) Tickle likes me to sing '*Where oh where oh where is Tickle?*' (to the tune of *Bobby Shaftoe*) as he's hiding under a blanket, and then he will pull the blanket off to reveal himself.

Food: Food is a great way of demonstrating your role as a nurturing adult, and is usually very motivating as an activity. If your child will accept you feeding them directly (as you might do a baby) then that can be a lovely bonding experience. If that is more difficult then you can introduce playful elements like putting hula hoops on your fingers, and letting the child eat them straight off, or put a doughnut on your finger and the child has to see how many bites they can take before it falls off. Another fun game you can play is to have two or three different little snacks and the child has to close their eyes or look away while you pop one in their mouth, then guess which one you have given them.

Jumping: Have your child stand on a pile of pillows or the sofa, and on an agreed signal they can jump off in to your arms. You can make this more of a challenge by adding one more pillow or cushion each time — hold them at first to help them get their balance though!

Crawling race: You and your child crawl on your hands and knees around a pile of cushions, as fast as you can, trying to catch each other's feet.

Newspaper punch: This is a fun Theraplay game which introduces elements of challenge. Hold a single sheet of newspaper in front of your child, stretched taught. When you give them a signal, the child punches through the paper. Make sure you're holding it firmly so it makes a satisfying noise! Then you do it again but with two pieces of newspaper, and so on. With all the leftover newspaper you can screw it up in to balls and then your child can try and throw the balls in to a basket you make with your arms.

Balloon races: Hold a balloon between you and your child (e.g. between your foreheads, shoulders, tummies etc) and see if you can move across the room without dropping it. You could place a big washing basket at the other side of the room and aim to drop the balloon in there. See if you can do it all without using your hands! Have a big pile of balloons and try and use a different body part for each.

Wheelbarrow races: Make a 'wheelbarrow' with the child — they have their hands on the floor and you pick up their legs, then they walk along on their hands. This is excellent for building core strength but just be aware it will be very tiring so you might have to build up the time you do this for gradually.

Sensory play: There are lots of different types of sensory play, as it covers anything that involves stimulating the senses. Try experimenting with different textures, colours, and smells, to see what your child enjoys — things like sand, water, bubbles, shaving foam, slime, glitter, sponges, stones, jelly, essential oils (mixed into water or foam, don't use these straight on to skin), fleece, silk, clay, playdoh, baking… the list is endless!

Teddy hospital: This used to be one of Fairy's absolute favourite games when she was little. Get a load of cheap plasters, micropore tape, bandages etc, and then sit with your child bandaging up their teddy bears. You can tell each other what happened to the teddy as you're putting the plaster on, e.g. 'This poor teddy bear fell over and bumped his knee, so I'm going to put a plaster on to keep it clean and safe.'

Tea party: Any games where you can be facing the child, such as having a dolls tea party, or doing some small world play (e.g. Playmobil) with them can be great for promoting positive interactions, and a bit less intense than some of the close up face-to-face games.

Jelly on a plate: This can be done as a face-to-face game, but it's such a lot of fun that even children who can't manage that might be prepared to try it if they are sat on your lap with their back to you. When you're singing or chanting the first two lines, bounce your child up and down a little, as you would do with a baby or toddler.

Jelly on a plate
Jelly on a plate
Wibble wobble, wibble wobble [wobble side to side]
Jelly on a plate

Biscuits in the tin
Biscuits in the tin
Shake them up! Shake them up! [big bounces]
Biscuits in the tin

Sweeties in the jar
Sweeties in the jar
Eat them up, eat them up [pretend to eat the child]

CAT McGILL

Sweeties in the jar

You can add other verses and movements, and maybe your child would like to make some suggestions. The key part of the game is building the anticipation between the gentle bounces for the first two lines, and the big movement in the third line; this again plays on the raising and lowering of anxiety.

5
Me

Communication theme: All about me
Social/emotional theme: Self-esteem

Song lyrics

Oh I may not be an astronaut who flies around in space
I won't win the Olympics, except the sleeping race!
I haven't got a unicorn to ride around the park
And I can't fly like Superman, or stop it getting dark

But never mind all that because I'll tell you something true
I'm the bestest me there is, and you're the bestest you!

I am amazing! I'm the very best!
I am just so wonderful, never mind the rest!
I am super brilliant, come on can't you see
I'm the most amazing, spectacular, wonderful, awesome, marvellous ME!

Background

This was the very last song I wrote for the album; I had a vague idea I wanted to do a song promoting self-confidence, but kept putting off writing it until the very last morning of recording. It's a really important subject though, so I'm glad I persevered.

Self-confidence is a funny thing. We all know that it's important to promote self-esteem in your children, but the thing that we perhaps *don't* think about so much is what needs to come before you even get to that point — the *self-concept*. Put simply, this is the ability to think about yourself as a person.

It can be helpful to think about the development of the self-concept in two separate stages.[15] The first stage is for the child to understand that they are a being that is separate from the world around them. Psychologists think that this can begin to develop from as early as 2–3 months old, and it happens very naturally as infants start to interact with the world and observe what happens — for example they smile at an adult, and the adult smiles back, or they push a ball and it rolls away. The second stage in the development of the self-concept is understanding that they are also an object in the world, and can have distinct properties applied to them, just as other objects can. In other words, they have understood that the ball they have just pushed is an object separate from themselves, and learnt to apply some descriptors to the ball, e.g. 'The ball is big' or 'The ball is red'. Next is the realisation that the 'self' can be described, or put in to categories in a similar way; usually the first categories to become internalised are age ('I am three') and gender ('I am a girl').

With these things in mind, it's easy to see how a child who hasn't had a lot of opportunities to interact with the world may not have been able to fully form their self-concept. Perhaps they spent a lot of time in a buggy or car seat, or weren't given any toys to hold or play with. When I read about this type of thing it always makes me think how much we are influencing our children's development without even realising it; like when your baby is grizzling and you give them your keys to play with, or you just chat to them as they make random noises at you. This multitude of small moments during a day will all be influencing how your child's brain develops, how their sense of self develops, how they will come to view the world and their relationship with it. That then makes for a really stark contrast with the children who *don't* experience those moments, and can help put in to

---

[15] Lewis, M. (1990), Self-knowledge and social development in early life, in L. A. Pervin (ed.), *Handbook of personality* (pp. 277-300), New York: Guilford, in McLeod, S. A. (2008), 'Self concept', retrieved from https://www.simplypsychology.org/self-concept.html on 18 June 2019.

perspective how much work we need to do now to fill in those gaps retrospectively.

Psychologists think of the self-concept as having three distinct parts to it:[16]

- The view you have of yourself, or the *self-image*
- How much value you place on yourself, or your *self-esteem*
- What you wish you were really like, or the *ideal self*

As we know, a person's self-image doesn't necessarily reflect reality. Your child may believe they are an inherently bad person, or they might not have much of a concept of self at all. I also find the concept of the ideal self really interesting, this idea that we have internalised a 'perfect' version of ourselves that we compare our real selves to. Some people might think about that quite consciously ('This is the sort of person I want to be, so this is how I'm going to behave') but for others it may be totally unconscious, and we may simply have this nagging feeling that we're not quite good enough somehow. If we feel like most of the time we're doing OK, that we are behaving and achieving more or less how we'd like to be, then we will most likely be quite satisfied with ourselves, have a relatively positive self-image, and sense of self worth.

If, however, we find ourselves sometimes behaving in undesirable ways, and not matching up to this 'ideal self' then we are likely to have poor self-esteem and a negative self-image. Psychologically it's a very uncomfortable state to be in, and can cause a lot of internal conflict. This can also be the case when we *perceive* our self-image as not matching up to the ideal self, even if other people would think differently.

---

[16] Rogers, C. (1959), A theory of therapy, personality and interpersonal relationships as developed in the client-centered framework, in (ed.) S. Koch, *Psychology: A study of a science, Vol. 3: Formulations of the person and the social context.* New York: McGraw Hill, in McLeod, S. A. (2008), 'Self concept', retrieved from https://www.simplypsychology.org/self-concept.html on 18 June 2019.

With this understanding of the self-concept, we can see why some children find it hard to accept praise (it conflicts with their self-image), why some children might internalise a great deal of shame in relation to their trauma-triggered behaviours (the behaviour conflicts with their ideal self, but they can't control it so believe therefore they must be a bad person), and how some children don't seem to have much understanding of themselves at all. There are no quick fixes for any of this, but as always, if we can understand where the behaviour is coming from then we can begin to work out ways to help.

Using the song

I wasn't sure initially whether I wanted to start off the song with all the things I *couldn't* do, but in all honesty, that's a common starting point for children so in the end I decided that was the way to go. It also means I can make the point that you can still be amazing, even whilst acknowledging your limitations. I've used silly and extravagant things instead of the day-to-day things children might find difficult; as you may have guessed by now I'm a big fan of using humour and silliness in my work to help cushion the potentially difficult feelings.

I've also very deliberately gone over the top in the '*I am amazing*' section, putting all of those positive words on the highest notes of the song, to make a statement and grab attention. I know some children will find this really difficult, but sometimes it's a bit easier to go overboard, ham it up a bit, as if you're not quite taking it seriously. It really doesn't matter whether you believe it or not, the song is simply putting the idea out there that it is possible to be positive about yourself.

When I sing this song with my children we have a good giggle at all the things we can't do (feel free to make up some of your own), and then I go full on theatrical for the last section, to make them laugh and keep the positive feelings at the fore, rather than the uncomfortable feelings where the self-image doesn't match up to this idealised self. Of my children it's often Fairy who finds this hardest, but with time and repetition I will gradually encourage her to join in with little bits of the song, maybe just a word or two at a time. I also sing it *to* her, so

ADOPTING A MUSICAL APPROACH

I'm changing the words to *'Fairy is amazing, she's the very best'* etc. If she finds that too difficult then I'll switch back to me, and say 'Oh all right then, I'll have to sing it about me instead!' and make her laugh again. This isn't something you can rush, and you'll have to make the judgement about how to tackle it with your own child.

Everyday life

There are plenty of things you can introduce in to your everyday life to help your child build a positive self-concept, many of them you may already be doing without even realising it. One of the most important things you can do is being mindful about how your everyday interactions and responses to things might affect your child.

One of the most simple things that has been talked about for years is to explicitly talk about the child's *behaviour* as separate from them — this works with both positive and negative comments. For example, instead of saying 'It's naughty to hit' you could say 'I don't like it when you hit me'. The first example could easily reinforce a child's negative view of themselves (I hit, therefore I am naughty), whereas the second doesn't make any judgement on the child themselves, but is a statement of your response to their behaviour. It might seem like I'm just nit-picking, but when you are parenting a traumatised child these things really do matter. Equally if you want to praise a child for doing something good, you could say 'I know you worked really hard to achieve that' rather than 'You're so good at that'. This helps the children to place a value on the work that they put in to something, rather than whether or not they are 'good' at something.

When I'm talking to Tickle about his behaviour I sometimes go even further to depersonalise it, so for example I might say 'Your arms are doing a lot of hitting today and it's hurting me'. I've also seen this used in Sarah Naish's *William Wobbly* series, and I think it's a really good way of acknowledging that the child doesn't always have full control over their trauma behaviours, and separating the child from the action. It gives them a way of thinking about their behaviour without inducing shame: 'My arms keep hitting and I don't really know why.'

Another therapeutic parenting technique encouraged by Sarah Naish is the use of natural consequences.[17] Natural (or logical) consequences are different from punishments; they don't attempt to shame a child in to better behaviour, they simply teach a child that there are consequences to all of their actions. Removing a privilege as a sanction can reinforce a child's idea that they are a bad person and deserve to be punished.

An example of this (sometimes very subtle) difference could be that Tickle gets cross and throws one of his toys out of the window. A punishment might be that I say he's now not allowed to play with that toy because of his behaviour, whereas natural consequence might be that well, the toy has gone out of the window, so now you don't have it to play with any more. It's the same outcome, just a slightly different spin on the situation; in the natural consequences scenario we don't attempt to place any blame, and we don't need to get cross or angry or attempt to 'teach the child a lesson'. Incidentally, we have a rule in our house that if a toy gets thrown then mum and dad will look after it for a while to 'keep it safe' — this is an example of a logical consequence. Again, there's no anger involved, we're simply helping keep Tickle's toys safe when he's not able to do so himself.

Sometimes a natural consequence of Tickle's behaviour will be that I get cross. Some people get very worried about getting cross or shouting at their children, but personally, I think it's totally normal to get cross with your children from time to time! When I do get cross with Tickle I try to avoid saying things like 'You've made me cross'; rather I'll phrase it as 'When you do that, Mummy gets cross' so there's no blame attached, only an action and a consequence. Showing your child that you can be cross with them but still love them is a great lesson, as is demonstrating how to say sorry and make up with someone when you've fallen out. I always say sorry when I have shouted at Tickle, even if it was absolutely necessary; if he was about to run in to a road and I've shouted in order to stop him, I will still apologise and explain why I shouted. The important thing is that no

---

17 Naish, S. (2016), *Therapeutic Parenting in a Nutshell: Positives and Pitfalls,* Amazon.

one is blamed or shamed for any behaviour; we are still good, lovable people even when we behave in undesirable ways.

One of the other easy ways you can teach your child about themselves is simply to talk about them — almost like a running commentary of what they're doing. A lot of parents find this comes quite naturally with young children; for example if you're building a tower out of blocks you might say something like 'Tickle has a big red block, that's going to be the bottom of the tower. Now we're looking for something to put on top of that, ah yes, that yellow one looks just right.' As well as helping with language development you are also giving a child a script for talking about and categorising different objects and things. You can do this with anything and everything; try and make a point of doing it when you're doing something to the child, like helping them to get dressed, or brushing their hair or teeth. You can also include likes and dislikes, perhaps when you're out shopping or when you're cooking 'Ooh I think I'll cook some parsnips with dinner, Tickle really likes parsnips, don't you'. If you feel a bit self-conscious about this, just remember that you are trying to help your child build up a healthy inner voice, and the way that you talk to them will likely become the way they learn to talk to themselves in the future.

Games and activities for developing self-esteem

Any of the games or activities in this book can help support your child's growing self-esteem; for example, being allowed to make a choice about something can help a child to feel like their opinion is valued. Below I've gathered a few more specific activities and ideas for developing a self-concept and improving self-esteem — and do also look at the face-to-face activities in chapter 10 (I will love you) as those will be really important for this topic.

I have linked to any specific songs and resources mentioned here from my website catmcgill.uk/AAMA-resources.

All About Me book: We made a very simple book for Tickle which had lots of photos of him doing various different things, with descriptive captions. It helped him to build up a narrative of who he is as a person (e.g. I like swimming, I like eating chocolate, etc). We also did a book about things Tickle is good at, again with pictures of him doing the different things. Very simple but it made a difference really quickly.

Achievement diary: At the end of every day, ask your child to think of three things they did really well, or that went really well, and write them down in a book. It doesn't matter if they're only tiny things, the idea is to build up a collection of positives that the child can look back on.

Special box: This is something I was taught years ago by a play therapist, and is essentially a really concentrated period of play where all your attention is on the child. It's based on Child-Parent Relationship Therapy, which is a whole programme of therapy and needs to be taught by an experienced Play Therapist, but this one little activity is something you can dip in to quite easily. The play therapist recommended setting aside a particular time each week to do this, and having a set collection of toys and games which is only used during this type of play (hence the 'special box' as it was named by Fairy). In your special box you need to have a variety of toys; some nurturing toys like dolls, play food, a doctors kit, some toys for more intense play like a bow and arrow, toy gun, or toy dinosaurs, and some creative toys like colouring pens, paper, cardboard boxes to make things out of, and stickers. Each time you do special box you set aside half an hour where there will be absolutely no interruptions, and the child is completely in charge of the play (unless they are going to do something physically dangerous in which case you obviously stop them). This means you don't make any suggestions for what they want to play with, you don't correct them if they say something wrong; the child is completely in charge and you do exactly what they tell you, no more no less. It's a similar idea to **Love Bombing**,[18] where the child is your total focus and takes the lead in all activities for a designated period of time.

Masks: For a slightly older child, you could make and decorate two masks, one mask they could decorate to represent how the outside world sees them, and one is how they see themselves. This could be used as an activity to prompt a conversation.

Role play: Dress up as kings and queens, and make some royal proclamations — what rules would you make if you were in charge of the country? Or dress up as superheroes, and talk about what superpowers you have.

Squiggles: Close your eyes and draw a random squiggle on a piece of paper. Ask your child what they think it looks like, or what they could make it in to, and encourage them to add to the drawing if they want to. Take it in turns to do random squiggles for each other to see what you can find in them.

Magic tricks: Help your child learn how to do a couple of simple magic tricks. It will really boost their self-esteem when they show you a trick and you can't work out how it's done.

Give them a job: This won't work for all children, but some children can feel really proud of themselves if they've been able to be helpful.

---

[18] James, O. (2012), *Love Bombing: Reset Your Child's Emotional Thermostat,* London: Karnac.

Tickle, for example, absolutely adores doing the recycling. For older children, you could give them a chore that is their responsibility, such as feeding a pet — though you may need to support them in doing it consistently. This can help children feel like you trust them to do a good job.

Make something together: A sense of shared achievement is a wonderful thing for a child's self-esteem. Get them to help you to make a cake, make dinner, make a model, plant some flowers in the garden, paint the fence, anything really as long as you are doing it together and you celebrate the achievement at the end. For older children it could be something that takes a bit more time and commitment, that they have to do over a few sessions.

Songs

Below are suggestions of songs you can listen to or sing with your children to promote positive self-esteem. You can just enjoy these as great songs, or use the lyrics as starting points for conversations (particularly with older children), by asking things like 'What do you think the singer means when they say…' or 'Have you ever felt like that?'

Good to be me: This is a simple song for younger children, and on the resources webpage I've linked you up to a Makaton signed version.

Believe: There are lots of songs with this name, the one I've linked to is by Lin Marsh, a fabulous children's songwriter. It's quite a popular song with primary schools so your child may already know it.

The climb: This song by Miley Cyrus is about perseverance, and appreciating the journey you take through life rather than just the things you manage to achieve.

Roar: This classic by Katy Perry is about having the confidence to stand up for yourself.

ADOPTING A MUSICAL APPROACH

Brave: This song by Sarah Bareilles talks about having the courage to speak your truth.

This is me: A hugely popular song from the film *The Greatest Showman*, this is about standing up for yourself and being true to who you are.

I can be: I came across this song while I was researching this chapter, and it's a really sweet song about believing in yourself. The video is lovely, and I particularly like the way it is full of children with all sort of different needs, and backgrounds.

We are the champions: Another classic by the legendary Queen. The whole family can sing along to this one!

Just the way you are: There are a couple of songs with this name, both on similar themes, but the more modern incarnation is by Bruno Mars. It has a fabulously feel-good chorus.

CAT McGILL

6
In my house

Communication theme: Telling you about myself
Social/emotional theme: Family set up

Song lyrics

In my house there's a big TV
And I've got a bedroom all for me
There's stairs and a shower and a sofa too
And an oven so clean it looks brand new

In my house
My house
My house

In my house I've got Daddy and Dad
To look after me when I get sad
They read me stories and they play with me
And they cook me lovely food for my tea

In my house
My house
My house

In my house I've got a blue front door
I like to zoom my cars all over the floor
There's pots and pans and a kitchen sink
And a washing basket full of clothes that stink!

In my house

CAT McGILL

My house
My house

In my house it's just me and mum
We get on fine, we're having lots of fun
Sometimes we play with Lego or we go for a walk
Or we cuddle up in a blanket and talk

In my house
My house
My house

In my house I live with Uncle Fred
He's got a big round belly and a shiny bald head
There's Aunty Dot and my cousin Ann
And a little black and white cat, who's called Sam

In my house
My house
My house

Some things in my house are the same as yours
We both have ceilings and we both have doors
Some things are different and that's OK
It makes it more interesting when you come to play

In my house
My house
My house

Background

When I was starting out with this project I asked other adopters on Twitter what subjects they would like to see covered, and different family set-ups was one suggestion that came through loud and clear. I did wonder whether it was something I could just incorporate in a subtle way, weaving it through the songs on the album rather than explicitly dedicating a song to it. After all, I thought, this is 2019 — do we really need to explicitly say that it's OK to be different? Unfortunately, it only takes one glance at the news to realise that yes, apparently we do. Representation is *so* important, and as a society we really need to normalise the fact that every family will look slightly different. Same-sex parents are valid. Single-parent families are valid. Kinship carers are valid. Disabled parents are valid. Mixed-race families are valid.

In My House is a song to celebrate the things we have in common, and acknowledge the things that we do differently. You might notice that I've included some fairly random things in the song, like ovens, stairs, and sofas; this is because I wanted to make the point that having different people living in your house should be no more or less remarkable than having a different colour front door or a stinky washing basket. It's just a different version of normal. I also wanted to draw attention to the fact that we can always find something we've got in common, and those things often far outnumber the differences.

I've built up this song using a simple line of melody for the first line of each verse, which I've then repeated at a slightly different pitch for the second line, and again at the original pitch on the third line. Repeated patterns like this are a common feature in Infant-Directed Speech (IDS).

The beginning of the last line of each verse gently rises in pitch; a rising contour in IDS can be used to indicate that it's the infant's 'turn', or as an encouragement to join in, so this acts as a signal that the chorus is coming up. For most of the last line I've stayed on that top note, to build the anticipation and excitement, before the release of the punchy chorus section '*In my house, my house, my house*'.

I really hope that this is a fun song that children can enjoy rocking along to, and helps them feel like their version of normal is perfectly OK.

Everyday life

The communication theme in this chapter is 'Telling you about myself' which follows on closely from the previous chapter on self-concept and self-esteem, and chapter 3, which was about storytelling and life story work. Although I've arranged things into topics in this book, none of this will happen in a vacuum, and you should feel free to pick and choose different activities from different parts of the book to suit you and your family.

It's important that your child can feel comfortable talking about themselves; their likes and dislikes, their body, their choices and preferences, and to be able to say no if the situation calls for it. This is so intrinsically linked with the self-concept, self-image, and belief that they are a person who is *worth* talking about, that if this is something your child finds difficult I'd recommend starting with some of the self-esteem activities in the previous chapter.

I once did some one-to-one mentoring work with a little boy in my daughter's class at school. He was six years old, with no identified learning needs, and yet when I started off with (what I thought would be) a simple 'getting to know you' activity, he wasn't able to tell me anything about himself other than his name and his age. Eventually I managed to find out a little bit about him by asking him a series of yes/no questions, but I wasn't able to get a clear sense of his family set up, or who he was as a person. I don't think he knew himself, really.

Unfortunately I wasn't able to work with this child for very long, but if I'd had a bit more time I would have been interested to find out whether this was an issue of not having the *language* to talk about himself, or not having the *concept* in the first place.

Some children do find it quite hard to talk about themselves. Many parents I'm sure will have experienced the after-school scenario where you eagerly ask what your child has done at school today and they respond with 'Dunno', or 'Can't remember'. When Fairy was little I used to get round this by suggesting silly activities that she might have done: 'Did you climb on top of the school roof? Did you go for a ride on a dragon?' When she would say no to each one I would pretend to be really exasperated and say 'Well what DID you do then?' and she'd eventually manage to remember that she'd read a book, or done some colouring.

When Tickle joined our family and both children were at different schools we used to play a tea time game where I would ask 'Who did maths today?' or 'Who had lunch today?' and they would have to shout out 'ME!' if they'd done the thing I said. Then I'd ask each in turn what they had done in maths, or what they'd eaten for lunch, or who they'd played with at break time. I also get much better answers from Tickle if I sing him the question 'What did you do at school today?'; he'll sing me the answer back using the same tune.

If your child can't *tell* you about their day, can they communicate it to you in another way? Can they draw it? Or show you through dance or sounds? Or perhaps you could try doing some small world play with them, and see what comes out? Doing some of the activities below (and from the previous chapters) will gradually help your child to build up their language skills, and hopefully help them communicate more confidently with you and other people.

Games, activities, and songs for telling you about my family

Below are a selection of games, songs, and activities; some are based on the communication theme of 'telling', and some are to do with promoting a variety of different family set ups. As usual if you go to catmcgill.uk/AAMA-resources then you'll find a list with links to the items you can buy, or to the songs I've suggested.

Telling

'Ask it, Tell it' cards: I first came across these when I was working as a learning mentor in a school; they are a set of cards with either an 'Ask' instruction (the person who picks a card has to ask a question to someone else) or a 'Tell' instruction (the person who picks a card has to tell the other people something). They work especially well in small groups.

I went for a walk: The leader starts with 'I went for a walk and I saw...' and then says something that they saw on a walk (e.g. a dog). The next person says 'I went for a walk and I saw a dog and...' and chooses their own thing, with each person adding something new so that the list builds up. You can let everyone choose their own thing, or have a bag or box of pictures or items that they can choose from (which can also act as a memory aid if you lay them out in the order they were picked in). You could adapt this to 'I went to school and I did...' if that's a conversation you want to encourage. Don't forget to add in some silly things to make everyone laugh!

Say something nice about...: This is a game you could play as a whole family. Write all of your names on individual pieces of paper or card, and put them into a jar or hat so you can't see which is which. Take it in turns to pick a name out and say something nice about that person. You can have some prompts prepared in case your child needs support with this, or a selection of words they can choose from to describe the person. If anyone picks themselves they have to say something nice about themselves, no skipping turns! If you want to you could write down all the nice things everyone has said and look back over them together at bedtime.

ADOPTING A MUSICAL APPROACH

I like to eat (apples and bananas): This is a fun song that I remember from primary school, where you use the vowels to create different funny sounding words. I've included it here because you can make up your own versions using different things that you and your child like to eat, and have a giggle at how funny the words sound with different vowels in.

A cat sat on a mat: This song is a nice alternative if you're a bit bored of *Old MacDonald*, and is a good song for younger children to practice telling you what they see. You can make up your own verses, or link in with pictures or photos (e.g. if our cats are sleeping on my bed, then Tickle and I might sing 'The cat sleeps on the bed' — it doesn't really matter if it doesn't rhyme, it's just about practising describing something, and conveying information to another person).

I went to visit a farm one day: Another *Old MacDonald* alternative. The version of this that I've linked to has a call and response section incorporated, so you can take turns with your child doing the animal noises and you copying them.

When I was one: Also known as the *Pirate song*. Your children can make up funny things for you to do at each age — they can be rhyming things, or not, it's up to you.

Family set-ups

The Great Big Book of Families: This book by Mary Hoffman was recommended to me; it's quite long but you can dip in and out of it and it can act as a prompt for starting conversations.

Two Mums/Two Dads: The author Carolyn Robertson has published a number of books about same-sex families, including *Two Mums, Two Dads: a book about adoption*, and *Two Mums and a Menagerie*.

The Family Book: I'm a huge fan of Todd Parr and all his resources, and *The Family Book* is another great one for celebrating different types of family.

It's OK to be Different: Another Todd Parr classic, this is one of my favourites.

Why do I have two mums? Asks Bryon: This is quite a sweet book, aimed at 5- to 6-year-old children, and carries the message that all families are special.

Heather has two mummies: I haven't read this one, but it's got some good reviews on Amazon and looks like it's aimed at children around 3 to 5 years old.

Mommy, Mama, and ME/Daddy, Papa, and ME: Again, I haven't read these but they have great reviews on Amazon. They are board books aimed at children aged around 3 to 7 years.

Who's in your house: This is a lovely, peaceful little song that covers both the 'telling' theme and the different family set ups, and was the original inspiration for *In My House*. It was written for children with communication difficulties, so it's quite slow-paced and has lots of thinking/processing time built in. You can adapt the words for your own situation.

Two Gay Papas: Not just one song but a whole collection! This is a collection of nursery rhymes and stories that have been adapted to feature dads — plus there are a couple of versions that have two mums in as well.

7
Socks

Communication theme: Routines and transitions
Social/emotional theme: Personal care/independence

Song lyrics

Can you put your socks on, socks on, socks on?
Can you put your socks on, all by yourself?

Can you put your shoes on, shoes on, shoes on?
Can you put your shoes on, all by yourself?
Or do you need some help?

Background

I'm cheating slightly by including this song here, as I didn't write it
during the project, but it is probably the song that we have used the
most with Tickle over the years so I really wanted to share it. As I've
said elsewhere, when Tickle first came to live with us sometimes
singing was the only way we could get him to do *anything*, be it getting
dressed, getting in the car, or eating his dinner.

The socks song came about because we'd been told by the social
workers that Tickle needed to practice getting dressed independently,
but it was something he still found quite tricky and often very
frustrating. In the early days I would sit with him and sing this song,
one verse for each item of clothing, round and round again until he'd
managed to put it on successfully. Then we'd start again with the next
item. If there was something that was proving extra tricky to get on
then I'd insert the 'do you need some help' line, to remind him that he

was allowed to ask for help if he was struggling; this was something that didn't always occur to him.

Structure and routine for adopted children

Routine is helpful for all children, and for care-experienced children particularly so. Routines help children to predict what is going to happen day-to-day, and moment-to-moment — something which is very important when you consider the upheaval and stress of a child being removed from their birth parents and taken to live with strangers.

Children, even children who live with their birth parents, often have little or no say in their daily lives; adults tell them that they have to get dressed, go to school, sit at the table, eat their dinner, have a bath, and so on. For children who feel safe and secure with their parents, that doesn't present too much of a problem, but for children who have learnt they can't rely on adults to consistently meet their needs it feels very scary to surrender control. It might sound like I'm contradicting myself here, as I've just said it's helpful for parents to set routines for our children; however it's important that we recognise why it can sometimes be difficult for them, as much as they may need it.

Creating a plan and structure for the day helps to show our children that we have thought about their needs, that we have planned in time when we're going to feed and nurture them, and that we are safe, capable adults. Some children will need a high level of detail so they can begin to feel safe enough to let the adults take charge (though be aware they may still resist it at times). For some children, having a detailed plan for the day can make the difference between being able to cope with it or feeling completely unsafe and becoming dysregulated. We have certainly found with Tickle that we need to plan things out much more than we'd ever expected, and changes to the routine, or introducing new places or activities can still be difficult even four years down the line.

In the early days of living with us, Tickle would wake up at 5.00am and need to know what he was having for breakfast, lunch, and dinner, and ideally what he'd be having the next day as well. He is much more able to be flexible these days, but routine is still a really big part of our lives, and a really important part of helping Tickle feel safe. It can be the little things like doing his morning jobs in a certain order, or there's a certain type of yogurt that he eats at breakfast time but not any other time of day; or it could be the bigger things like knowing what we are going to do each day of the school holidays, or what we're having for dinner. (If you want a resource to help with holiday planning, adoption blogger Hannah Meadows has a free template downloadable from her website — also linked from my resources page.)

Visual timetables

Visual timetables can be a great resources for children who need a bit of structure and routine; we use these in a few different ways and Tickle finds them really helpful.

At school Tickle has a timetable with what he's doing each day, and each activity has a photo of the adult who is going to be with him for that activity. On the whole he has one adult assigned to him for the day, but they obviously have timetabled breaks and lunchtimes, so he always has someone different during those times. Tickle's teacher sends home the next day's timetable every night, so he can look through it and see who he's going to be with for each part of the day. Tickle can't read yet, but he can recognise symbols, so he has learnt to 'read' his timetable by looking at the symbols for each subject.

If I'm honest, we're not really organised enough at home to make the best use of the visual timetable we've got here, but it's there for the days when we need it most. There are two sections of it that are fixed — morning routine and evening routine — and everything else in between is on a strip of velcro so we can adjust it each day. We use a mixture of Makaton symbols and photos, and everything is laminated to help it last a bit longer. Even when we're not using it, Tickle quite likes to play with it, and make up games about what he's doing each day.

We've also done emergency visual timetables, if we've been having a tough day when we're somewhere other than home. For example, we were at Gran's for Christmas one year and Tickle was having a difficult day and worrying about when we were having food, so Gran hopped on her computer and made up a timetable for the day using clip art. We made sure it had plenty of snack times scheduled, as well as play times in between snacks — on that day Tickle really needed that level of detail.

If a full day's timetable is a bit much, another option is to do a 'Now' and 'Next' board. This will have a photo or symbol for what is happening now, and one for what is happening next, which you move along or take off the board as you change activity throughout the day.

I've linked to a visual timetable template from my resources page; on the same site there's also resources for getting ready for school, daily routines, and now and next templates. You can find this at catmcgill.uk/AAMA-resources under the 'Socks' section.

Using routine songs in everyday life

Many parents will use songs to manage everyday activities, and songs written expressly for this purpose are sometimes known as routine songs, transition songs, or 'marker' songs, as they are used to mark a particular activity. There are a few different ways you can use these songs:
- To keep the child engaged and motivated during an activity
- To help a child wait and/or prepare for the next activity
- As signals for an activity starting or coming to an end

Songs to engage

Many parents already make use of songs to keep their children motivated during a repetitive activity, for example singing '*This is the way we brush our teeth*' whilst you are helping your child to clean their teeth. We find with Tickle this helps him to understand how long the activity is going to be happening for; he can tell whereabouts in the song we are, and knows that when the song finishes the tooth brushing is over. He also really enjoys music and singing, so for him it's a great way to keep him engaged.

I also use songs for washing and drying hands, as that's something Tickle will often forget if he's in a hurry or can't really be bothered. We've made the drying hands one in to a fun game, where I will sing *'This is the way we dry your hands'* (to the tune of *Here we go round the mulberry bush*) but instead of the *'cold and frosty morning'* for the last line, I sing *'Dry, dry your…'* and then pick a random body part to tickle with the towel. I have really fond memories of doing this with Tickle at his foster carers' house during introductions; he was really taken by the idea, and approaching it in this playful way made it easier for him to accept my help with personal care routines. Washing and drying hands became an enjoyable time for us to bond rather than a chore. These days Tickle is very familiar with the song and the game, so I will leave a big pause at the end and let him pick the body part for himself.

Songs for waiting

Tickle used to find car journeys absolutely unbearable; he had no idea how long he was going to be in the car, and needed a lot of reassurance from Husband and myself about where we were going. When we drove him back to our house from his foster carers' for the last time we sang for the entire journey — well over an hour. I usually use my old favourite *Here we go round the mulberry bush* for impromptu car journey songs; you really don't need to worry about using the same tune for everything, in fact a familiar tune is often better, as the child will already know the association and understand what is expected of them. I tend to use the mulberry bush tune in any situation where Tickle will be expected to slow down, wait, be patient, or take his time doing something.

During a car journey we will use the mulberry bush tune in a variety of ways. Firstly *'This is the way to Gran's house, to Gran's house, to Gran's house'* to remind Tickle where we are going, and reassure him that we know how to get there. Secondly, we'll sing *'We're nearly there, we're nearly there, we're nearly at Gran's house'*, as a bit of variation, and then *'Here we are, here we are…'* when we are just arriving. He finds the familiarity of the song very reassuring, and will often start singing it himself if he's getting restless.

Songs as signals

Song can be a really good way of preparing a child for the end of an activity and the start of a new one, as well as a motivating factor during the activity. When I am running my SEN singing group for example, we have a particular song that we always start and finish the session with — when we start we sing it as a hello song, and at the end of the session we sing it as a goodbye song. For the children who don't have such a strong grasp of language, the musical cue can help them to orient themselves. Adam Ockelford has done some great work on the use of musical patterns with children with profound and multiple learning disabilities, visual impairments, and autism, showing that these children can both understand that musical patterns are linked to a certain meaning, and reproduce them in order to communicate.[19]

You don't have to be a professional singer or have a huge repertoire of songs in order to make use of them in this way. You can use any old melody and make up whatever words you need; for younger children nursery rhymes like *London Bridge is falling down* or *Twinkle Twinkle Little Star* are great starting points for simple, repetitive melodies. For slightly older children you could use something like *Frére Jacques*, or American military call and response chants (*I don't know but I've been told*) or even pick out songs they like from films. Again, you can make up the words to suit whatever you need at the time — I've been known to sing '*Let's go home, let's go home, can't stay here any more!*' to the tune of *Let it go* from *Frozen*.

Children will generally find it hilarious to hear you misappropriating their favourite song in this way, and they're much more likely to view whatever instruction you're giving them in a favourable light if you've given them a bit of a giggle first. I've given a few examples on the next

---

[19] Ockelford, A. (2018), *Tuning In Music Book: Sixty-four songs for children with complex needs and visual impairment to promote language, social interaction, and wider development*, London: Jessica Kingsley.

page to show how I might use well-known tunes to create new routine songs.

CAT McGILL

Songs to support routines

Below are a selection of songs to support routines and transitions throughout your day. If you go to catmcgill.uk/AAMA-resources you will find a page linking to all of these resources so you can check out any you are not familiar with.

Here we go round the mulberry bush: This is probably the most well-known routine song, and can be adapted for any activity you like.

Here we go round the mulberry bush, the mulberry bush, the mulberry bush
Here we go round the mulberry bush on a cold and frosty morning

This is the way we brush our teeth, brush our teeth, brush our teeth,
This is the way we brush our teeth on a cold and frosty morning

This is the way we comb our hair/put on a coat/eat our breakfast...

I don't know but I've been told: As I mentioned before, you can use this American military chant to make a fun routine song for kids who are less fond of nursery rhymes. On the resources page on my website I've linked to a soldier version so you can hear what it sounds like in its original form, as well as a couple of alternative versions. You can have a go at making up your own version, or try this bedtime chant I came up with:

I don't know but it's been said (I don't know but it's been said)
It is nearly time for bed (It is nearly time for bed)
When we finish this old song (When we finish this old song)
It's time to put your PJs on (It's time to put my PJs on)
Upstairs (Upstairs)
Brush your teeth (Brush my teeth)
Story time (Story time — yeah!)

You could even just keep it to a couple of lines, and use it as a signal:

I don't know but I heard say (I don't know but I heard say)
Time to put your toys away (Time to put my toys away)

ADOPTING A MUSICAL APPROACH

It's time for dinner: I found a sweet little dinner time song on YouTube, which I've linked from my resources page. I love it because it's so simple and repetitive, and you could easily use it as call and response, with everyone singing together on 'yummy' at the end of each line.

Rumbly in my tumbly: An old one, I know, but if your children like Winnie the Pooh then have a look at this song Pooh sings when he's climbing the tree to steal the honey from the bees. (You don't have to sing the bit about climbing trees and stealing honey if you don't want to encourage that sort of behaviour.) Tickle likes me to sing this when he's getting impatient for dinner.

Food, glorious food: Depending on your family's sense of humour, you might enjoy singing *Food, glorious food* from the musical *Oliver* at dinner times — but I'll leave it up to you whether you want to link the feast or the gruel section to your own cooking!

Tidy up songs: A quick search on YouTube will find you dozens of different tidy up songs. My favourite is one I learnt from a baby music group when Fairy was small, which is sung to the tune of 'Heads, shoulders, knees, and toes':

Now it's time to tidy up, tidy up
Now it's time to tidy up, tidy up
We're finished now, we've had enough
Now it's time to tidy up, tidy up

As I've said, you can also make up your own very easily. Here's an example of a tidy up song that I just made up on the spot, to the tune of *London Bridge is falling down*:

Now it's time to tidy up, tidy up, tidy up
Now it's time to tidy up
Play time's finished

And to the tune of *Frére Jacques*:

Time to tidy, time to tidy
Tidy up, tidy up
Put the toys away now, put the toys away now
Pick them up, pick them up

Don't forget it doesn't need to be complicated, or musically polished. Familiar, repetitive, and catchy is always best. And while we're talking tidy up songs…

A spoonful of sugar: The original tidy up song! Mary Poppins was way ahead of her time. Obviously this one is a bit more involved than my ones above, but if your children are fans of the film this could be a great motivator for them.

Washing/bathtime songs: Again, you can have loads of fun making up your own versions of well known songs. How about trying this to the tune of *If you're happy and you know it*:

If you're dirty and you know it, have a bath! [or wash]
If you're dirty and you know it, have a bath!
If you're dirty and you know it then your mucky face will show it
If you're dirty and you know it, have a bath!

Or this to the tune of *Sing a song of sixpence*:

Time to have a bath now, time to have a wash
First we run the water, splishy splashy splosh
Rubbing scrubbing here, and rubbing scrubbing there
And when we've finished on your body then we'll wash your hair

Or to the tune of *London Bridge is falling down*:

Now it's time to have a bath, have a bath, have a bath,
Now it's time to have a bath, let's get splashing!

ADOPTING A MUSICAL APPROACH

You could even use *Heads, shoulders, knees, and toes* as a bathtime song, washing each bit of your child as you get to it in the song.

Getting dressed: As an alternative to the Socks song, if you're helping your child get dressed you could use the tune of *The farmer's in his den* to sing:

We're putting on your socks
We're putting on your socks
Here we go, oh here we go
We're putting on your socks

Or to our old favourite, *London Bridge*:

Now we're putting your socks on, your socks on, your socks on
Now we're putting your socks on
Then your jumper [or whatever item of clothing comes next]

CAT McGILL

8
Jump

Communication theme: Giving/following instructions
Social/emotional theme: Emotional regulation

<u>Song lyrics</u>

Now here's a song to cheer you up when you are feeling down
Let's get your body moving and we'll turn your mood around

We'll start by stepping side to side
Then raise those arms and lift them high, and

Jump! When you're feeling sad, and
Jump! When you get mad
When your body feels wrong
Listen to your favourite song, and jump!

Let's get your body moving now we're clapping to the beat
Try and lift your knees up and then you can stamp your feet

Now bend right down in to a squat
And stick your bum out quite a lot(!) and

Jump! When you're feeling sad, and
Jump! When you get mad
When your body feels wrong
Listen to your favourite song, and jump!

Come on everybody now it's time to do the twist
You swing your arms and shoulders round and shake your hips like this

Now stretch your arms out nice and wide
And touch each knee on the other side, and

Jump! When you're feeling sad, and
Jump! When you get mad
When your body feels wrong
Listen to your favourite song, and jump!

Stretch up high then touch your toes
One more time before we go

Now crouch down low right to the ground
Listen for that happy sound, and

Jump! When you're feeling sad, and
Jump! When you get mad
When your body feels wrong
Listen to your favourite song, and jump!

Background

When I first set up *AAMA* as a project I ran a Kickstarter campaign to raise some of the funds I needed to do the recording, and offered a variety of rewards to people who were interested in backing the project. One of the rewards was to choose the theme of a song on the album, and this was chosen by adoptive mum and former foster carer Becky Brooks. Becky asked for a song to do high intensity activity to, maybe with instructions as part of the song — and *Jump* was the result.

The communication theme for this chapter is about giving and receiving instructions, but the overriding theme is emotional regulation — because of course you need to be emotionally regulated in order to give or receive instructions successfully. If we're going to really understand what emotional regulation is and how to achieve it, it helps to understand what the *opposite* looks like, and what can cause that state of *dysregulation*.

ADOPTING A MUSICAL APPROACH

Our nervous system

The nervous system in our body is what connects our brain to our heart, lungs, and other organs. The nervous system exists in order to keep you alive, and is almost entirely automatic in its functioning; you don't need to consciously remind yourself to keep your heart beating, or to digest food for example. It can be vital for our survival that we react quickly to threats, so if there is something in the environment signalling danger then your nervous system doesn't give you time to think, it acts on your behalf to keep you safe. If you think back to hunter-gatherer times, if you spotted a wild animal about to attack you, you wouldn't really have time to stop and decide on the best course of action.

Recent theories in this area suggest that there are three main parts to your nervous system.[20] Most people will have heard of the fight/flight system; this is an automatic response to danger, and is the system that would come in to play to make you run away from that wild animal you've just spotted in the undergrowth. Polyvagal theory refers to this as the *mobilisation* system — in other words, you can move your body to either run away from the threat or try to fight it. If fight or flight isn't an option however, then your *immobilisation* system will come in to play, meaning you may freeze, dissociate, or play dead. This is our most ancient danger response, evolutionarily speaking, and it's really important to remember that it's not a conscious choice we are making — the body will simply shut down in order to survive. When you are in this state, when your body thinks you are in danger and is making decisions for you outside of your conscious control, we would call this a *dysregulated* state. In other words, you are not able to consciously regulate or control your emotional state.

In an ideal world, we don't spend much time in those danger zones. According to polyvagal theory, our 'default' system for when there is no threat detected is the *social engagement system*, so named because it is the social clues from the other people in our immediate environment that are letting us know that we are safe. We subconsciously read cues

---

20 Porges, S. (2011), *The Polyvagal Theory*, New York: WW Norton & Company.

such as people's facial expressions, tone of voice, and body language, and our body interprets them, based largely on our past experience. When our nervous system considers us safe, the social engagement aspect (which is the more sophisticated part) will suppress the danger responses so that we stay *regulated* and in control of our responses.

To summarise: our 'calming' system is the *social engagement system*. In order to remain in a calm and regulated state we need safety signals from our social environment; meaning that facial expressions, gestures, and talking are really vital for helping a child feel safe. If the social engagement system detects a threat, then our first port of call is the *mobilisation* system — fight or flight. If fight or flight has not been possible (either on this particular occasion, or if a person has experienced ongoing traumatic situations where they haven't been able to get away) then our last line of defence is the *immobilisation* system, where a person may dissociate, freeze, or withdraw into themselves.

The problem for a lot of children who have experienced the care system is that their body has learned to be extremely fine-tuned to potential threats in the environment. Imagine that there's an insect buzzing around the room; I might hardly notice it, but my friend Fred who is allergic to bee stings and has previously been taken to hospital after being stung would instantly be tuned in to the sound of the buzzing. In this scenario, Fred's mobilisation system might come online in case they need to make a quick getaway, which might make them appear panicky or jumpy — or Fred may be so frightened that they simply freeze. These are all extremely useful responses *if the situation is dangerous*. Our children respond the way they do because *their bodies are reading the situation as dangerous and are acting to keep them safe*.

The role of music and dance

One of the best ways of reaching out to a child's social engagement system (the system of safety) is through music and movement. As I've said in the chorus of *Jump*: '*When your body feel wrong, listen to your favourite song, and jump!*'. Moving to music will allow the child to experience their mobilisation system (i.e. the movement) whilst also connecting with their social engagement system — even more so if they are dancing with another person. It's healthy and useful for a person to be able to move in and out of their mobilisation system whilst staying regulated; a good example of when this can be utilised is an athlete feeling nervous before a race and using the adrenaline to boost their performance. If your child tends to get really dysregulated with too much movement then look for ways that you can engage with them socially — with your voice, your facial expressions, gestures, and body language — to help them feel safe.

As we talked about with *Hide and seek*, a child's arousal levels are repeatedly raised and lowered during play. It's the job of the adult in this interaction to communicate with the child's social engagement system by maintaining a positive facial expression and playful tone of voice, in order to signal to the child that they are safe. Over time, the child will learn to manage the raised arousal levels without going in to a fight/flight state. You may need to keep a close eye on how your child is responding to the situation in the first instance, and always be prepared to take a step back and go more slowly if they are showing signs that they're finding it difficult. It's really important that they stay with the safe feeling, and gradually learn to tolerate more arousal without their body flipping in to their danger systems.

I had an opportunity to experience this myself just this morning; Tickle was wanting to play a hiding game, where we would take it in turns to hide under a blanket and sing '*Where oh where is Tickle/ Mummy/Dad*'. Tickle had a small Playmobil girl that he called Ellie in his hand, and my husband suggested he might like to hide her, which he did, but then became quite dysregulated as we were singing the 'where' song. The second time we hid Ellie he again became dysregulated, so I stopped the song, and showed him where Ellie was under the blanket. Then I said I was going to hide her again and Tickle could take the blanket off to find her, which we repeated two or three times. Husband 'wondered' out loud whether Tickle was worried because when we hid Ellie it felt like we were taking her away. We talked about this a bit, and reinforced that Ellie was Tickle's toy, and we won't take her away. We hid her again a couple more times and let Tickle take the blanket off straight away to find her — it felt important that he was the one who removed the blanket, to reassure him that he was capable of taking control and getting his toy back. Then we tried the song again, and this time Tickle was able to stay regulated while Ellie was hidden.

The main musical feature of *Jump* is the rising melody line that I've used throughout. In Infant-Directed Speech, a rising melodic contour is used to grab attention and encourage the child to join in, so that's what I've built in right through the song.

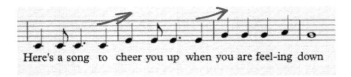

Here's a song to cheer you up when you are feel-ing down

Using the song

Jump acts as something of a pair with the song *Bubbles* (chapter 11) as they are both songs to aid emotional regulation; however they go about it in different ways. *Jump* is for those times when you need to do something energetic and get your body moving, and *Bubbles* is more useful when you need to calm down and take some deep breaths. Some people might prefer one or the other, or you might use both but in different situations. It doesn't really matter how you do it, use whatever works for you and your family.

With *Jump*, you've got the option of simply dancing along however you like, or following the instructions that are in the song. You can use it like you would in an exercise class and repeat the movement in time to the music, or just do the movement once, as it's described. Most of them should be self-explanatory, but there is one that I struggled to get clear in the song — '*Stretch your arms out nice and wide, and touch each knee on the other side*' refers to a cross-crawl: when you lift up your left knee and touch your right hand to it, and then lift up your right knee and touch your left hand to it. (It was hard to get that in to the song and rhyme it as well!)

ADOPTING A MUSICAL APPROACH

You can use the structure of the song to help your child to stay regulated; there is potential for them to get a bit overexcited during the chorus (jumping!) so you can use the verses with their clear instructions to engage with your child and bring their arousal level down. If you are both doing the moves together this will help you connect with their social engagement system and help them feel safe. If they are finding it a bit too much they might like to hold a teddy bear or toy, and make the toy do the jumping and follow the instructions for the movements.

CAT McGILL

Songs for active children

Below are a selection of a few more songs that you can use to burn off a bit of excess energy, as well as to practice following instructions, and staying regulated while having fun. All the songs are linked from the webpage catmcgill.uk/AAMA-resources to make it easier to find the ones you don't know.

For younger children

Shake my sillies out: I learnt this song at primary school in the early 80s and it's still going strong; it's a fun and active song to sing for those who have a bit of excess energy.

Everybody says sit down: This is a song I found in the book *Playsongs* by Sheena Roberts, and it works really well for toddlers and younger children. You can sit down during the first verse, and then jump up and dance in the second.

Hop little bunnies: A favourite of every single toddler I've ever met, this is a great song for those who like to jump around, but you can also really draw out the sleeping section so they stay 'asleep' for longer. The contrast of the two sections is great for practising the calming down needed to stay regulated in the active section.

Dingle dangle scarecrow: Similarly to *Hop little bunnies* this is another great one with 'sleeping' and active sections.

Kangaroos like to hop: A great little action song, another one I first got from *Playsongs*. Kids will love joining in with the actions.

Five little monkeys: Another fun jumping song! This is also good for supporting numeracy as you count down from five monkeys to one.

Come dance with me: Another dancing song with instructions, this one is in a call and response style. This song can also be good practice for asking questions and saying yes or no.

ADOPTING A MUSICAL APPROACH

Shake break: A fun lively song that younger children will enjoy dancing along to. The video I have linked to from my resources page is performed by muppet-like characters.

Body boogie: A funky song with dance moves that use different body parts one at a time.

Do the twist: Another fun song using different body parts. Useful for practising rights and lefts.

<u>For older children</u>

Time Warp: *The Rocky Horror Picture Show* may or may not be your cup of tea, but in my humble opinion the *Time Warp* is a cracker of a song, and I have many happy memories of dancing along to this as a teenager.

Watch me: This is a hip-hop song from 2015 by an artist called Silento. It's got some interesting moves, and apparently became something of a YouTube phenomenon as people uploaded their own dance video interpretations of the lyrics.

Cha cha slide: Another hip-hop song, released in the late nineties with an aerobics video type of vibe. It has dance instructions throughout, and kids will love the funky groove.

Tootsie roll: This 'brand new dance for 1994'(!) had me giggling as I was researching songs for this chapter. It's a pop/hip-hop song, which is a little dated but I think children will enjoy it nevertheless.

CAT McGILL

9
Don't worry Ted

Communication theme: Feelings
Social/emotional theme: Change/new places

<u>Song lyrics</u>

I love to go away on a fancy holiday
I always take my teddy bear, we're best friends all the way
This time we're off to France, where children love to dance
And stuff themselves with croissants if you give them half a chance

I don't want a fuss, so we're going on the bus
It's time to put your coat on, I'll carry all the stuff

I know it feels strange, and you don't like the change,
But we'll have fun you'll see
So don't worry Ted, I'll tuck you in to bed
And you'll be safe with me

I love to go away on a fancy holiday
I always take my teddy bear, we're best friends all the way
We're off to visit Wales to hear exciting tales
Of dragons in the mountains using sheep to shine their scales

It isn't very far so we're going in the car
Make sure you take your coat with you, the weather's quite bizarre!

I know it feels strange, and you don't like the change,
But we'll have fun you'll see
So don't worry Ted, I'll tuck you in to bed

CAT McGILL

And you'll be safe with me

I love to go away on a fancy holiday
I always take my teddy bear, we're best friends all the way
We're on a trip to Greece, to sunbathe on the beach
And climb up the Acropolis to see the view beneath

The car broke down again so we're going on the train
We'd better pack your coat just in case it looks like rain

I know it feels strange, and you don't like the change,
But we'll have fun you'll see
So don't worry Ted, I'll tuck you in to bed
And you'll be safe with me

I love to go away on a fancy holiday
I always take my teddy bear, we're best friends all the way
This time we're off to Spain, where we'll be entertained
By swimming, sun, and shopping, and siestas in the shade

The car would never float so we're going on a boat
Mind you don't get splashed now, where have you put your coat?!

I know it feels strange, and you don't like the change,
But we'll have fun you'll see
So don't worry Ted, I'll tuck you in to bed
And you'll be safe with me

I understand you'll moan, 'cos you don't like the unknown
We'll only stay a week or two and then we're going home

I know it feels strange, and you don't like the change,
But we'll have fun you'll see
So don't worry Ted, I'll tuck you in to bed
And you'll be safe with me

ADOPTING A MUSICAL APPROACH

Background

I wrote this song while we were away in the Lake District doing the first recording session for the *Adopting a Musical Approach* album. Tickle found it incredibly difficult being away from home and staying in a different house; usually when we go away we're camping so at least the tent is familiar, regardless of where we pitch it. Being in a different house was really triggering for him, and he was anxious almost the entire time we were there.

As with a lot of the songs on the album, I felt this fear of change would be quite a challenging topic to address directly in a song that's supposed to be light-hearted and fun. To counter this, I've introduced the idea of a teddy bear as the one who is feeling worried, which allows the child to take the role of comforter rather than having to directly identify with the uncomfortable feelings themselves. Being a step removed from the difficult feelings in this way could also help the child identify strategies that would help the bear feel better, in a way they might not be able to do when they are experiencing the feelings themselves.

Musically speaking, it was the chorus section of this song that I worked on first. I started with the line *'Don't worry Ted, I'll tuck you in to bed, and you'll be safe with me'*; I knew I wanted to finish it off with the melody gently falling in pitch, as in Infant-Directed Speech (IDS) this is used to comfort and soothe.

and you'll be safe with me

The U-shaped contours (starting high, going low, and then high again) like the ones I've used for *'Don't worry Ted'* and *'I'll tuck you in to bed'* are used in IDS to invite activity, so what I wanted to achieve in that section was to draw the child in to the song in order to be soothed.

Don't wo-rry Ted

The first half of the chorus ('*I know it feels strange and you don't like the change, but we'll have fun you'll see*') does the same job of drawing the child in, and with the rising melody of '*we'll have fun…*' elicits attention, letting the child know there's something interesting coming up, and encouraging them to join in and have a go at singing themselves.

we'll have fun you'll see

I've used the same U-shaped pattern as the backbone of the verses, to keep the link between the chorus and the rest of the song, and to make the most of that up and down type of melody that is so good for calming the nervous system.

A pathway back to safety

In the last chapter we looked at emotional regulation, and a theory of the nervous system called the Polyvagal theory. Stephen Porges, who developed the theory, has a great quote that epitomises what I want to talk about in this chapter:

'*Those who are bold and seek novelty are those who have the most efficient pathway back to safety.*'[21]

---

21 Porges, S, in 'Why the vagal system holds the key to the treatment of trauma' from the National Institute of the Clinical Application of Behavioural Medicine, http://www.nicabm.com.

ADOPTING A MUSICAL APPROACH

Porges is talking here about emotional safety, about feeling safe in your own body, rather than having a particular place or location that is safe, but it works in much the same way. We could take the quote very literally and think about being in the middle of a big, dark forest — I expect you'd feel much happier exploring along the big wide paths that are signposted than trying to find your way through the undergrowth. What Porges means by his quote is that children who don't know how to get to an intrinsic feeling of safety within their own bodies are going to really struggle to deal with anything unfamiliar or different in their environment.

It might be helpful at this stage if we think back to what we know about attachment behaviours in infants. We know that securely attached infants use their parent as a 'safe base' from which to explore the world, and a 'safe haven' when they need comfort.[22] Their life experience has taught them that their parent will always be there if something goes wrong — they are confident in their pathway back to safety.

Children who haven't had the experience of an attuned and responsive adult meeting their needs are starting from a very different place. They can't rely on anyone else to keep them safe, so their brains and nervous systems are constantly on the alert for potential dangers nearby. Every new situation is an additional stress, because they have to reassess each environment to work out whether they are safe. All children will have this to an extent — but most children will have learned to seek comfort from a trusted adult to help them deal with these feelings. Our children aren't able to do that; that's simply not how their brain works.

This will be a familiar struggle for many adopters and foster carers, as we know that our children often have enormous difficulties with going somewhere new, or doing something differently.

---

22 Hoffman, K., Cooper, G., Powell, B, (2017), *Raising a secure child,* New York: The Guilford Press.

Managing change in everyday life

It is an oft-heard cry on adoption Twitter, as adopters lament the fact that they used to have a varied and interesting life but now only ever go to the garden centre and soft play. We know from experience that keeping things predictable is really beneficial for our children, but what can we do when we *need* to introduce something new, or go somewhere different?

Feelings and expectations

Accept that it's going to be difficult. Accept that there will be fallout, and it will probably come when you're tired and grumpy. Make sure you plan in a couple of easy days after a big change, so that you've all got some time to decompress.

Accept that your child's feelings are completely valid, and for them, a completely logical reaction to something that their nervous system perceives as potentially dangerous. They are not deliberately being difficult, this is how their brains and bodies are wired.

It's important that we hear and validate our child's feelings, so try to avoid phrases like 'Don't be silly, there's nothing to worry about', no matter how tempting it might be. Instead try things like 'Gosh it must be exhausting to be so worried all the time. I can really see how worried you are about this. Is there something I can do to help you feel better?'

If your child finds it difficult to talk about their feelings, you might want to try a basic feelings board, where they can point to a picture or symbol that represents how they feel. If they find it too difficult when asked directly, you could introduce it by saying something like 'Sometimes children have a lot of different feelings when they have to (do this thing we're doing). Some children might feel happy, some might feel sad...' etc. Pay close attention to your child's reactions, notice if they perhaps look at one picture for longer than the others, or breathe differently, or make a sudden movement or shift their body when you get to that feeling. If you have a suspicion you could say 'I wonder if you might feel angry/sad/frightened' and see whether they will confirm it. My first experience using a feelings board was with Fairy when she was about five and was struggling with the idea of me and her biological father being divorced. We were reading a book called *Dinosaur's Divorce* which had a double page spread of feelings in the middle. With a bit of encouragement Fairy picked out 'ashamed' as the emotion she most identified with, which took me completely by surprise. It turned out that she thought she was the only person who had divorced parents, so we were able to talk about other children she knew who were in the same situation.

As I learned that day, it's useful to bear in mind that your child may have different expectations or worries that you may not have considered — when going on holiday they might be worried about whether there will be any toys in the new house for example, or whether they will be allowed breakfast. They may not know whether they are coming home again (halfway through our first holiday Tickle asked me if we still lived in our house). Your child may be used to going to different houses and having to suddenly learn a new set of rules, get used to new people, different meal times, and different expectations. They may not realise that you are going with them on holiday. Whenever our family are going somewhere new Tickle always likes to check whether there's going to be food, and whether there's going to be a toilet.

Preparation

One thing to think very carefully about is how much notice will you give to your child about the proposed change in routine? It's likely they will need time to process it, but sometimes too much advanced warning can result in even more anxiety, especially if the child only has a loose concept of time and how long they actually have to wait. There's no hard and fast rule for this, you will have to see what works best for your child.

One of the things Tickle and I like to do in advance of going on holiday is googling the local area, and finding out what sort of things there are nearby that Tickle likes — mostly soft play, parks, slides, and swimming pools. Sometimes we can get on Google Earth and actually see pictures of the place we're going to, or there may be photos on local websites. If it's somewhere we've been before I will show Tickle the photos of when we were there last time.

Social stories are another good tool for use in this sort of situation. A social story is simply one that describes an everyday situation that a child will experience. For example, a social story about going on holiday might look something like this:

'One day, Tickle and Mummy and Daddy decided to go on holiday. Mummy and Daddy found somewhere really nice to pitch the tent, with toilets and a playground just nearby. Mummy, Daddy, and Tickle will drive there in the car. When we get there we will cook dinner on our camping stove, and go to sleep in the tent.'

The story can be as long or as short as you need it to be; it can be just words, or you can add photos, drawing, or Makaton symbols to aid comprehension.

<u>Routines</u>

Bear in mind that your child may need even more routine or structure than normal when you are away from home. I've talked in chapter 7 about visual timetables, and these can be really helpful when you're away from home. We regularly go on holiday to Folk Camps, which are family-friendly holidays with a community music ethos at their heart. My kids love Folk Camps, not just because of all the music and dancing, but also because they are very predictable. No matter where you are in the country, you know there will be a table in the hall or marquee with squash and hot drinks available all day. There will be a table where you can do your washing up. There will be a noticeboard where the plan for the day is itemised. The children know that they can find the caterer right after breakfast and they will be able to tell them what's for dinner that day.

Folk Camps are all about community, so everyone mucks in with the cooking and cleaning to make the camps run smoothly, and Tickle

ADOPTING A MUSICAL APPROACH

loves helping out with little jobs like washing up and recycling. I have been going to Folk Camps since I was a small child and I cannot recommend them highly enough for families who would appreciate a little bit extra structure and support on holiday. If you want to find out a bit more then have a look at folkcamps.co.uk.

If camping or folk music isn't your thing, I'd still recommend planning out your days (and meals) so that your children know what to expect. You could also have a visual countdown of how many more days are left until it's time to go home, or try some of my routine songs from chapter 7 (Socks).

CAT McGILL

Songs and activities for coping with change

Below are some suggestions of games, songs, and activities that might help you to manage feelings around change. I have linked to any specific resources or songs from my website catmcgill.uk/AAMA-resources. You might also want to look at the routine songs in chapter 7 (Socks) as these may be helpful to provide some structure.

If you're happy and you know it: This is a great song for helping children learn to structure emotions. You can adapt the lyrics in this song depending on what you want to achieve, for example if you want to promote more positive strategies for dealing with big feelings then you could use something like 'If you're angry and you know it ask for help', or 'If you're angry and you know it hit a pillow'.

The feelings song: This is a sweet, slow-paced song that I found on YouTube. It's got a gentle calming feel to it, and it would provide a good conversation starter for some different feelings, and how you might feel in different situations.

Emotions song: It may not surprise you to know that there are many dozens of songs on YouTube about feelings. I particularly like the video for this one as for each emotion there are children making the faces to go along with it — this is good practice for reading facial expressions, and also a chance to have a go at making them yourself. This song also covers a wider range of emotions than in most songs, and includes things like confused, nervous, loved, proud, and jealous.

Sad, bad, terrible day: This may or may not be your cup of tea; I think it's a bit like the equivalent of 'I woke up this morning, and I was feeling blue…' but for kids! It might be a good one to have up your sleeve if your child needs someone to empathise with them.

Elmo and Chris from *Sesame Street* sing about feelings: I always love *Sesame Street* for the way it deals with a variety of issues, so I've linked you up on my resources page to this song where Elmo is learning all about feelings.

ADOPTING A MUSICAL APPROACH

Worry eaters: My children both love their worry eaters, which are soft toys with a zipped pocket for a 'mouth'. The idea is you can write or draw your worries and them put them inside the worry eater who will look after them for you.

Inside Out: This film is a little beyond Tickle just yet, but it was really helpful for Fairy when she was learning about her emotions, and gave her a useful way of viewing them as something separate from her conscious mind and therefore something that she might be able to influence. We could talk to her about how Fear had 'taken control' in her brain and it gave her a concrete reference to make thinking about it all a bit easier.

William Wobbly **books**: I've mentioned these before, but the William Wobbly series by Sarah Naish is really good for helping children examine the feelings behind their behaviours.

Songs about going on holiday

The idea of these songs is to give a positive reference point for going on holiday, reinforcing that it's a normal thing for people to do and that it can be a fun and positive experience.

Summer holiday: I couldn't really leave this one out: Cliff Richard's classic feel-good holiday song.

We're going to Ibiza: I realise it's an odd juxtaposition, suggesting Vengaboys right after Cliff Richard, but this is another great feel-good song about going on holiday.

Island in the sun: If your family are rockers rather than popsters then you could try Island in the sun by Weezer. It's a pretty chilled out song and the video has lots of cute animals in.

Shotgun: It's not necessarily immediately obvious, but George Ezra's Shotgun is about going on holiday, sitting back in your car and watching the scenery go by, feeling contented. I've never yet met a child who doesn't like this song.

Homeward bound: A song about being homesick. Not quite in the theme of positivity I grant you, but just as important to acknowledge the sad feelings as well as the positive ones.

10
I will love you

Communication theme: Feelings
Social/emotional theme: Unconditional love

<u>Song lyrics</u>

Once there was a little girl, her name was Annabeth
She lived at home with mummy, and a goldfish she'd called Geoff
But Anna had a secret fear, and in the dark in bed
She'd wonder who will love me?
Who will love me?
Round and round inside her head

Anna was a lovely girl, so very kind and sweet
But sometimes she'd get angry and get itchy in her feet
And then her feet would kick things, and then mummy would get sad
And she'd think who will love me?
Who will love me?
Who will love me when I'm bad?

But Annabeth was lucky, 'cos she had a clever mum
Who saw behind the kicking something else was going on
She got Anna's favourite blanket and wrapped her up so tight
And whispered 'I will love you'
'I will love you
Every day and every night'

Anna's mummy cuddled her and held her very tight
She said 'Sometimes you get angry, and sometimes you want to fight
But I will never leave you, no matter what you say

CAT McGILL

I promise I will love you
I will love you
Every night and every day'

Everyone gets angry sometimes, everyone gets sad
It's OK to be worried, and it's OK to get mad
But if you're ever wondering, or feeling insecure
Remember I will love you
I will love you
I will love you ever more

Remember I will love you
I will love you
I will love you ever more

Background

Being separated from your birth parents is a horribly traumatic thing, and it's little wonder our children have such big and difficult feelings to contend with. Many children struggle with these feelings to the extent that they can become physically or verbally aggressive with parents and siblings, which often then results in even more feelings of guilt, shame, and sometimes a real fear that their behaviour will lead to them being rejected again. For a child who has been let down by the adults who were supposed to be looking after them, trusting another adult is a big ask. They may worry that they're going to have to move on again, or they might think it was their fault that they can't live at home, and feel that it's inevitable they will be sent away from you sooner or later. Some children who feel like this might try and push people away, or 'test' the new adults in their life to see how much they love them. Will you still love me if I swear at you? Will you still love me if I hit you? Will you still love me even if I show you all of these big, horrible feelings that I've got inside?

I wrote this song a response to some of those questions. I wrote it all in one sitting, one afternoon; it just seemed to flow out like it was just waiting for someone to pluck it out of the air and write it down. Through most of the album I have been quite cautious about broaching topics directly, and have used stories or metaphors instead; however for this song it felt right to go straight in and address it head-on. As it turns out, it has ended up as one of Tickle's favourite songs on the album, and if he's dysregulated this will often calm him instantly.

This song holds a very special place in my heart. We know that love on its own is not enough, but love is the foundation. Love is the reason I'm sitting here writing this while I wait for Tickle to get home from school. Love is the thing that held our family together when we were at breaking point. If there is one thing I want to say to Tickle, that I want him to really hear, and believe, it is this: I will love you, always.

The social engagement system

We've been talking a lot in the last few chapters about the different branches of the nervous system, and the one I want to focus on in this chapter is the calming system, which in polyvagal theory is known as the social engagement system.[23]

The social engagement system is quite a new development in terms of the evolution of our species; reptiles don't have one at all, it's only found in mammals. It's a very fast system, so messages get passed around our body extremely quickly. The nerves in the social engagement system connect up an array of muscles in our face and head with our hearts and the rest of our nervous system. Porges calls this the 'face/heart connection'. If you think about someone who is depressed, you'd expect them to have quite a flat-looking face, perhaps droopy eyes, and you'd expect them to speak slowly, and perhaps with a lower pitch to their voice. Porges would say that the face (and voice) is reflecting the state of the heart, in other words, our face communicates to other people how we are feeling inside.

As well as communicating to people how we are feeling inside, the primary role of the social engagement system is reading signals from

---

23 Porges, S., in 'Why the vagal system holds the key to the treatment of trauma' from the National Institute of the Clinical Application of Behavioural Medicine, http://www.nicabm.com.

other people in our immediate environment, and communicating this to the rest of our nervous system. This is why it's really important to think about how we act around our children, as their nervous systems are likely to be primed to pick up danger responses — we need to use our face, body language, and tone of voice to help project signals of safety to our child's social engagement system. The key part to this theory is that it's a *social* engagement system; the path to calming and regulating the nervous system comes from interacting with another person. In other words, the way you learn to regulate your own emotions is from someone else helping you to do it first.

We see this all the time with young babies, who cannot regulate their own emotions. When a baby cries or screams most adults would instinctively rock them, speak gently and soothingly to them, maybe sing to them or rub their back. The adult is activating the baby's social engagement system in order to calm and sooth them. We see it also in over-emotional toddlers; the adult will get down on to the child's level so they are face to face, speak soothingly to them, make eye contact, and touch or hug them. The adult is helping the child to regulate their emotions, via their social engagement system. You can see how, with consistent and loving care, over time a child's brain will build the pathways to allow them to calm and soothe themselves — and hopefully you can also see how a child who *hasn't* had that input will almost certainly lack the ability to do so.

We know that when we care for children who have experienced trauma and neglect we have to parent in a way that fills in their developmental 'gaps', and one of the main ways we do this with the social engagement system is through face-to-face play. Some children may find this too intense at first; they may be experiencing triggers or flashbacks (perhaps they had an abuser who always smiled before the abuse started) or it may just be that they can't allow themselves to be vulnerable enough to trust that the signals they are reading from you are really safe. If this is the case then it will take a lot of time, and a lot of patience. If you do have a child who can't manage face-to-face games, you will still be able to connect with their social engagement system through your tone of voice; using a gentle sing-song voice to speak to them will help to send calming signals. One interesting thing to note is that being in a fight/flight state causes changes in the activation of the middle ear muscles, meaning that when you're in the fight/flight state your hearing is extra sensitive to low frequency sounds, the sounds the body interprets as dangerous[24]. If you're a man reading this, it might be worth being extra mindful of your tone of voice when speaking to a frightened child, and try to keep your voice as light and melodic as you can.

If your child can tolerate and enjoy face-to-face play, there are some ideas on the next page you might want to try. As always, keep a close eye on your child's responses, and if they become dysregulated or anxious then stop straight away. The aim whilst playing these games is for your child to feel absolutely safe at all times, and start to make some positive associations between the way that you interact with them and the feelings of safety. Face-to-face play can be so powerful, as it allows you to reflect the child's emotional state back to them, and seeing their emotions reflected by you is the first step in learning to understand and manage them.

---

[24] Porges, S., in 'Why the vagal system holds the key to the treatment of trauma' from the National Institute of the Clinical Application of Behavioural Medicine, http://www.nicabm.com.

Games and activities for face-to-face interaction

In this chapter I've concentrated on face to-face games and activities that will help you and your child spend some time very close together, learning about each other, and interacting with each other in a fun and curious way. You want your child to know that you are fascinated by them, so lavish your attention on to them as much as possible.

If you think these will be a bit much for your child then chapter 4 (Hide and seek) has other games for building attachment that are less about intense face-to-face interaction and more about being playful together, or chapter 13 (Who) has games that focus on nurture and the body. I've linked all the songs from my website catmcgill.uk/AAMA-resources so you can look up any that you're not familiar with.

Beep: Press your child's nose and say 'Beep!'. Try gently touching other parts of their face or body to 'see what noise they make', and invite the child to touch your face, making various different noises as needed. Tickle could spend hours playing this game.

Pop cheeks: Inflate your cheeks with air and help your child to 'pop' them with their hands or feet. You can add funny noises to this for extra giggles!

Stickers: Put a colourful sticker on your child's face or body, and let them put a matching one on you in the same place. Take it in turns to be the one who chooses where the sticker goes, and the other person has to match it. Before you take the stickers off, touch the matching stickers together, nose to nose, elbow to elbow, etc.

Kissing games: Not all children will like being kissed, so do go carefully with this one; I usually ask Tickle if he wants a kiss, and also *where* he wants it. You can have fun with Eskimo kisses (rubbing noses) or fairy kisses (fluttering your eyelashes on to your child's cheek).

Cotton wool ball stroking: Have your child rest in your arms and gently stroke their face, arms, and hands with a cotton wool ball or a piece of soft material. You can softly describe the features you are touching as you go if you like, or you could ask them to close their eyes and then tell you or point to where you touched them.

Copycat/mirroring: This is a simple game — the adult copies everything the child does, as closely as possible. It can be noises, making faces, dance moves, or anything else. This is a hugely powerful game for a child, as it shows the adult is totally focused in on them; they quite literally see themselves mirrored back by your actions.

Make a face: On the theme of mirroring, ask your child to make a sad face/happy face/excited face/cross face, and then copy it back to them as best you can. This works particularly well with quite young children, and helps them to reflect on their emotions.

Don't laugh!: Make funny faces or noises to try and make your child laugh, while they try to keep a straight face, then swap over so they try and make you laugh.

<u>Songs</u>

Row, row, row the boat: Tickle often talks about playing this during introductions, so it obviously made a big impression on him. You can either do it face to face with the child, or with another adult sit on the floor and use your legs to make the 'boat' and have the child sit 'inside' it facing one of you. All join hands and 'row' back and forwards as you're singing.

Row, row, row your boat
Gently down the stream
Merrily, merrily, merrily, merrily,
Life is but a dream

Extra verses:

Row, row, row your boat
Gently down the stream
If you see a crocodile
Don't forget to scream!

Row, row, row your boat
Gently down the river
If you see a polar bear
Don't forget to shiver

Row, row, row your boat
Gently to the shore
If you see a lion there
Don't forget to roar

Rock, rock, rock your boat
Gently to and fro
Merrily, merrily, merrily, merrily
In to the water you go! (SPLASH!)

Hand-clapping games: You can use basic hand-clapping games to get in some face-to-face time with young children, such as *Pat-a-cake* or *A sailor went to sea*. With older children see if you can remember any of the more complicated ones we used to do on the playground at school — or if that wasn't you then a quick Google search will throw up loads to learn! *Double double* is quite a good one for older kids.

Pat-a-cake, pat-a-cake baker's man
Bake me a cake as fast as you can
Pat it and prick it and mark it with B
And put it in the oven for baby and me

A sailor went to sea, sea, sea
To see what he could see, see, see
But all that he could see, see, see
Was the bottom of the deep blue sea, sea, sea

Double double this this
Double double that that
Double this
Double that
Double double this that

ADOPTING A MUSICAL APPROACH

For *Double double* you have a different clap for each of the words 'double', 'this', and 'that' — usually one is clapping both hands with your partner, one is clapping the backs of both hands with your partner, and one is making a fist and bumping fists with your partner.

Jack in the box: This little song is a nice variation on peekaboo that works for toddlers and slightly older children. Start by sitting on the floor and with your legs make a 'box' for the child to sit in, facing you, and lift them up and down as you reach those parts of the song.

Spots spots spots: Another song I got from the excellent book *Playsongs* by Sheena Roberts. As you're doing the rhyme, cradle your child with one arm, and use the other hand to gently touch imaginary spots all over them. In the tiger part, stroke your finger in long stripes. You could even make up your own verses.

Open, shut them: This is a lovely little finger play song/chant which works really well with toddlers and young children. You can either do it face to face, or with the child sat on your lap and their hands in yours, so you're making the movements together.

Open, shut them [open and shut your fingers]
Open, shut them
Give a little clap
Open, shut them
Open, shut them
Lay them in your lap

You can then swap in '*Give a little clap*' and '*Lay them in your lap*' for '*Give a little shake*' and '*Keep yourself awake*' — or you can make up your own version.

CAT McGILL

11
Bubbles

Communication theme: Pausing
Social/emotional theme: Emotional regulation

Song lyrics

I love blowing bubbles
See them floating on the breeze
Let's blow them all around
Don't let them touch the ground
Can you count with me?

Let's blow some bubbles! Are you ready?
One... two... and a really big one: three...!

I love blowing bubbles
Right up in to the sky
I don't really know
How far each one could go
Let's blow them really high!

I love blowing bubbles
Two watch them swirl and soar
You think they'll never stop
When suddenly they pop!
We'll have to blow some more

I love blowing bubbles
So wide and far and free
If I really blow

Who knows how big they'll go?
Let's try it now and see

I love blowing bubbles
Their colours really shine
Come stand here next to me
We'll blow one each and see
If yours is as big as mine

I love blowing bubbles
And what fun this has been
Let's watch them float away
We're finished for today
And now it's time for tea

Background

In my head I always think of this song as a pair with *Jump* — both are songs that can be used to manage emotional regulation, but they go about it in very different ways. Whereas *Jump* was designed to get you up and moving, *Bubbles* is all about pausing to take some very deep breaths. It does sound like it's something your mum would tell you to do when she gets annoyed with you, but there is a scientific reason that deep breathing is so good for calming you down; your heart rate actually slows down slightly when you breath out (this is known as Respiratory Sinus Arrhythmia). Taking some long, slow breaths out can really help to calm your whole nervous system down; but as we know, it's not always as easy as that with children, so sometimes it can be helpful to have something up your sleeve for when you know they need to regulate but they're not in the mood for sitting quietly.

Emotional regulation is the theme I want to come back to with this song. *Jump* is a high-energy song that aims to help children to safely experience their mobilisation system whilst staying regulated, however *Bubbles* is all about lowering the energy levels, breathing, and being still. Really, that's the ultimate expression of feeling safe — being able to 'immobilise without fear',[25] or in other words, feeling safe enough to be 'still' in the presence of other people.

We had an interesting experience playing with bubbles during one therapy session. Tickle really loves bubbles, and would keep asking me to blow them towards him, but every time I blew some he would suddenly panic and say he was frightened. Our therapist thought that he was experiencing a raised arousal level in his body (because it was a fun game) that he was misinterpreting as fear, rather than as excitement. Tickle hadn't yet learnt how to manage these raised levels of arousal that happen during play without them triggering his panic systems. With lots of smiling, happy voices, and reassurance from us and from our therapist, Tickle started to explore the concept of excitement, and gradually began to relax and enjoy playing with bubbles — as you'll hear evidence of on the album. When I was writing the song *Bubbles* I used lots of gently flowing up and down curves in the melody, which are found in Infant-Directed Speech when the parent wants to maintain regulation or reward behaviour.

let's blow them all a - round don't let them touch the ground

As we learned in the previous chapter, there are muscles in the middle ear that are directly connected up into the calming part of your nervous system (the system in your body that keeps you alive), which helps to explain why some types of music can have an almost instant effect on your mood. This type of flowing, up and down melodic contour that I've used in *Bubbles* is really soothing to the nervous system as it mimics the type of speech pattern we use to convey calm and safety.

---

[25] Porges, S., in 'Why the vagal system holds the key to the treatment of trauma' from the National Institute of the Clinical Application of Behavioural Medicine, http://www.nicabm.com.

Deep breathing

I mentioned in chapter 8 that your nervous system is almost entirely automatic, but breathing is the one part of it that we have some conscious control over. The ability to control our breath is a hugely powerful tool that can allow us to tap right in to our nervous system and regain control of our autonomic responses. As our breath slows, and our heart rate slows, this sends a strong signal to our nervous system that we are in control and we are safe.

Tickle has been practising taking deep breaths to calm himself down for some months now, and he's got really good at it. The majority of the time it will only take him 3–4 breaths to be back in control of himself, and I have even witnessed him doing it spontaneously, without any prompting. There are times when he finds it much more difficult, when his nervous system has been really triggered and he needs help from an adult to be able to bring it back under control. At times like this I usually introduce a little game to help motivate him to do the deep breaths — usually I pretend my finger is a candle that he has to blow out, but he has to blow a really long and steady breath otherwise the 'candle' just flickers but doesn't go out fully.

The power of the pause

From a communication point of view, being able to pause and be silent is a really important skill. You can't have an interaction based on turn-taking (like a conversation) if one person isn't able to manage pausing to let the other person speak. This can be tricky for some children, and if we consider how difficult it can be for children to 'immobilise without fear' then we can see why this might affect their ability to interact with others in this way. You can help children with this by introducing small pauses in to games and everyday interactions, for example if you're playing a tickling game, start by creeping your fingers towards the child, and maybe making a slow, rising 'oooh' sound before you suddenly tickle them (assuming that your child is happy with this type of game). You can gradually extend the creeping build up, and your child will learn to enjoy the anticipation. You may need to do this a lot so that your child feels comfortable enough with the predictable part of the game (I will be tickled and it will be fun) to be able to tolerate the waiting. As always, if your child seems dysregulated then stop, and slow things down.

If your child doesn't like tickling there are any number of other ways you can introduce this same technique. Games like peekaboo, for example, work really well. I would always advise using a vocalisation during the pause to reassure your child that you haven't disengaged from the game, and you're still there with them, as this could potentially be a trigger for children who have experienced neglect. You could even use the power of the pause when faced with a choice about something such as food, toys, or games — take your time choosing, but make sure you exaggerate your vocalisations so your child knows you are still connected. 'Hmmm, I wonder what flavour of ice cream I fancy today? Hmmm.. let me think…' Again, start small and gradually build up the tolerance.

Using the song

Bubbles has a break in between each verse where I encourage you to take some deep breaths along with me, and pretend to blow some bubbles. You can blow imaginary bubbles if you like, or you could get some bubble mix and blow real ones. The breaths are the most important part of the song, with the verses in between just there to provide some structure and a soothing melody. I wouldn't be surprised if some children will need support to stay focused on the song and the deep breaths, so don't worry if they only manage a couple of verses. Using real bubbles would probably help them to engage more with the song, but make sure you encourage them to take long, steady breaths rather than short, hard ones.

Games and activities for deep breaths and pausing

Here are a selection of songs, games and activities that make use of breathing, silence, or a pause. These can be great for children who need practice at impulse control, so if that's relevant to you then just make sure that it's you who gives the 'go' signal when it's time to do something — you can gradually build up the time that you're asking them to wait. Don't forget that all the songs are linked from my website if you need to look any up: catmcgill.uk/AAMA-resources

Deep breaths

Cotton wool ball games: There are loads of fun games you can do involving balls of cotton wool that make use of deep breathing techniques. If you want you can blow through a straw, or just do it without.

1) You and your child hold a wide scarf between you, and blow a ball of cotton wool back and forth. Alternatively, have the cotton wool ball in your cupped hands, and blow it to the child's cupped hands, like a game of catch.

2) Lie on the floor on your tummies (also great for building core strength) and blow cotton wool balls back and forth between you, trying to get one past your partner, or under their arms.

3) Make a racetrack on the floor with two pieces of string, and have a race to see who can blow their cotton wool ball all the way down the racetrack quickest. You could add in some obstacles for a bit of extra challenge.

Balloons: Blowing up balloons is obviously great for deep breathing. You could let them go and watch them zoom all around the room before blowing them up again, or pinching the neck of the balloon to let the air out with a screechy noise. Or, you might enjoy making balloon rockets — I've linked to a video from my resources page to show you how.

ADOPTING A MUSICAL APPROACH

Balloon keepy-uppy: See how long you can keep a balloon in the air just by blowing on it — no touching allowed!

Milkshake bubbles: Blow bubbles through a straw into a milkshake — see if you can get them all the way to the top of the glass.

Candles: Light some candles and blow them out. Try moving further away from the candle, and see how far away you can move and still manage to blow it out. You could also try blowing gently to see if you can make the flame flicker but not go out.

Ping-pong balls: Put a ping-pong ball in to a glass, and see if you can blow it out again. Try taller glasses for more of a challenge.

Feathers: Blow gently on to a feather and watch it shake. Try blowing up one side and then down the other side. Can you blow on your feather to make it float up in to the air?

Maltesers: Lying flat on your back, place a Malteser on your lips, and see if you can blow it up in the air. If you want to be really clever you can try and catch it in your mouth and eat it. Or, see how long you can keep a Malteser in the air for. This is a really fun game and very motivating, as you might imagine!

Lion breath: There is a yoga pose called 'lion' where you take a really deep breath in, and then breath out hard with a harsh 'Ahhh' sound and stick out your tongue. I've linked to a video of what it looks like from my resources page.

Tummy breathing: Have your child lie flat on their back, and place a cuddly toy or beanbag on their tummy. They have to try and make the toy go up and down as they take their breaths.

Sesame Street: *Sesame Street* have a song called *Belly breathe* which I've linked to from my resources page. They also have a brilliant app called *Breathe, Think, Do* which is designed to help children take some deep breaths and work out solutions to a selection of problems. It's aimed at preschool children, but I used it with Tickle until he was six or seven and he found it really useful.

Lung capacity: Older children might enjoy measuring their lung capacity. You can do this as a simple experiment at home using a large bottle, some hosepipe, and a big bowl of water. I've linked to a video on my resources page which shows you how to do it.

Mindfulness/meditation: You might want to try a guided meditation for children, or some mindful breathing. Fairy has a guided meditation from Relax Kids that she really likes — I've linked to their downloads page from my website.

<u>Pausing</u>

The beanbag game: Place a beanbag or toy on top of your head. Have your child place their hands ready to catch, and on an agreed signal, tip the beanbag off your head for them to catch — everybody has to wait for the signal before doing anything. If they need help with the catching you can put your hands under theirs to guide them. Take it in turns to balance the beanbag and catch it.

Toilet paper bust out: This is another brilliant Theraplay game. You wrap the child's legs, arms, or whole body with toilet paper or crêpe paper, and they have to wait for your signal to break out of it. If your child is nervous or hesitant then have someone else do it to you first so they can see, and when they are ready to have a go themselves then just start with their hands. This is a really good exercise in regulating yourself enough to wait.

Musical statues: The ultimate pausing game: dance around to your favourite music, and when it stops you have to freeze until the music starts again.

Stop: This is a cute little song I found on YouTube when I was researching this chapter, which includes a chorus section where you stop and then start again.

ADOPTING A MUSICAL APPROACH

Dance and freeze: A funky song, on a similar premise to *Stop* above, but probably cool enough for slightly older children to enjoy.

It's oh so quiet: This song by Björk is a lovely demonstration of how you can take the energy right down in a song. If your child likes this song you could sing it together round the house, and practice drawing out the pause before the loud section, as described above.

Uptown funk: My kids love this song. There's a big 'stop' section in the middle which you can use to practise your freeze, and there's also loads of opportunity to practice call and response turn-taking type interactions with the interplay between the main vocals and the backing singers.

CAT McGILL

12
Chat away

Communication theme: Conversation
Social/emotional theme: Permanence

Song lyrics

Chat, chat away
I love to chat all day
To tell you all the things I've done
And games I love to play

Chat, chat away
I love to chat all day
But mummy's ears are filling up
And now she needs to say

Shhhhhhh...

Background

This is supposed to be a slightly tongue-in-cheek song for those times when your ears are just so full up of chatter you would give almost anything for five minutes of peace and quiet! Tickle doesn't quite take the hint yet, but Fairy has cottoned on and I only have to start singing this for her to giggle and roll her eyes at me.

Of course, many children (some might say all) will chatter away at length to whoever will listen, seeking connections with other people, and learning about the social world we live in. With children who have suffered the trauma of being removed from their birth family however, it can be useful to look a little bit deeper in to what might be going on.

We've been discussing the nervous system in the last few chapters, and in particular the social engagement system, so in that context it is completely understandable that children might need an ongoing connection with an adult via their social engagement system, in order to continue to receive the signals that let them know they are safe. For children who have been neglected, left on their own, or experienced an absent or emotionally distant caregiver this will be even more important. It's very easy for adults to say that the child is now in a safe environment — but that doesn't mean that the child feels safe. Their body and brain have developed to give them the best chance of survival in the environment they were in, and that is not going to change overnight, it's literally hard-wired in to their brain and nervous system.

Permanence

Most people who've been around adoption for a while are familiar with the word permanence, but I thought it would be quite useful to think about how it means something slightly different for adults and for children. For adults involved in adoption and fostering, it means finding a safe and stable home for a child; their forever home and their forever family. It means the social workers have done their jobs, and that child (hopefully) will not need to move again but can stay settled with one family. For adults, in a way, it's an ending: job done, permanence achieved.

You won't be surprised to hear that it's a bit more complicated than that for children. When we think about what permanence might mean to a child it's useful to think about how it is defined in psychological terms: the understanding that something or someone continues to exist even when they can't be seen.

ADOPTING A MUSICAL APPROACH

In psychology it's usually referred to as object permanence, and will typically develop in a child at around 4–5 months old.[26] It's at this stage that they will search for a toy hidden under a blanket, reach for something they have dropped from their high chair, and start to find peekaboo absolutely hilarious. It's also at this stage that they can start to experience separation anxiety. They have a firm mental concept of their caregiver as a distinct and separate person, so can become very anxious when they are out of sight.

When you think about permanence from that point of view, you can see that even a baby of only a few months old will be fully aware that it has been left alone, or that it has been separated from its mother, and then its foster carers. Permanence then, by this definition, brings with it the weight of the loss you have experienced.

It's now very easy to see why a 'forever home' doesn't give a child an instant feeling of belonging and security. Loss and separation are woven right through the fabric of adoption, and we do our children a disservice if we can't acknowledge that. You have to wonder as well, what this experience of loss does for a child's sense of object permanence? They know that things do continue to exist when you can't see them, but that is not their experience when it comes to people. Indeed, for children who don't have any contact with their birth families or previous foster carers, it might really feel like 'out of sight, out of mind'.

We had a little glance in to Tickle's experience of this recently, when Gran went away on holiday. Tickle loves Gran, and we live fairly close so he sees her quite regularly. When Gran went away on holiday for a week, she brought back presents for both children, and Tickle was initially perplexed. 'Why has Gran brought me a present?' he kept asking. I explained that it was because Gran had been on holiday, but he still didn't understand. So I told him that Gran had been away on holiday, and we had been at home, so she hadn't been able to see us for a while. While Gran was away, I said, she was thinking about you

---

26 McLeod, S. (2018), 'Jean Piaget's theory of cognitive development', retrieved from http://www.simplypsychology.org/object-permanence.html on 7 July 2019.

and she missed you, so she brought you this present to let you know that she was thinking about you, even though she was away on holiday and we were here. Tickle was utterly delighted with this idea. He leaped around the room shouting 'Gran was thinking about me!' and flapping his hands. Tickle continued to mull over this idea during the next few days, and brought it up a few times in conversation, always with a note of pride in his voice.

Managing separation in everyday life

It's a fact of life that your child will have to deal with being separated from you many times over the course of a day — when you go to the toilet, or to sleep, for example. I expect there are people reading this thinking 'Ha! Not even then!' and I very much sympathise! Even now Tickle will still sometimes prefer to sit on a stool outside the bathroom while I go to the loo, though not as much as he used to. Being able to tolerate these small separations will really help your child feel calmer and more secure, so it's worth thinking about how we can help them learn to do that.

For me, there are very few problems in life that can't be improved upon by singing a song, but in this case it can be a really powerful way of maintaining that connection with your child's social engagement system even when you are out of their field of vision. I saw something on Twitter a long time ago (I forget who said it so apologies for the lack of credit) about an adopter who used to sing loudly the whole time she was on the toilet, so that her child could feel reassured she was still there.

You can use some of the activities and songs around pausing from the previous chapter to start to build up your child's tolerance of silence and stopping, and games like peekaboo work really well for young children to introduce the concept of a safe separation from a caregiver. You may need to build this up really gradually, and keeping the sense of fun and safety through play and social engagement will be really vital.

ADOPTING A MUSICAL APPROACH

Games and activities for safe separation

Here I've suggested some games, songs, and activities that will help you introduce the idea of a safe separation and help build up your child's tolerance. Remember it's important that the child feels safe at all times, so if you sense they are becoming upset or dysregulated then stop the game, and don't be afraid to go back a few steps so you can move forward more slowly. Any specific resources or songs listed below, can be found linked from my website catmcgill.uk/AAMA-resources.

Hide and seek: Hide and seek is the perfect game for managing separation anxiety in a fun way. The games from chapter 4 (Hide and seek) will also be useful, as they will help build a bond with your child, and the more secure your child feels in your relationship, the easier they will find it to separate from you.

Hello, goodbye: This is a Theraplay game that's another way of playing peekaboo. Your child sits in your lap, face to face, while you support their back with your hands. Say 'hello', and then lean the child backwards whilst saying 'goodbye. Then bring them back up and say 'hello' again. You can also do this while standing, with the child's legs around your waist, if they are small enough. The idea is that you go out of the child's line of sight, but you are obviously still there touching them and speaking to them, and there is a predictable pattern of going away and coming back.

Stuck together with glue: Take a pot of imaginary glue, and pretend to use it to 'stick' you and your child together. You can have fun trying to do things whilst stuck together, like tie your shoelaces or make a drink. Let your child take the lead on how they want to manage the game — they might enjoy the closeness, or they might want to unstick straight away. If you can, let them be the one to decide when it's time to unstick.

Tin-can telephones: Try making a 'telephone' out of tin cans (or paper cups work fine too) and string, and go into a different room from your child to talk to them through it. Or you could buy a set of walkie-talkies and practice being in separate rooms from your child whilst still being able to talk to them.

Long hugs: If your child seems to need a lot of attention, then you could try saying 'Oh no, have you run out of hugs? Let me fill you up again!' and then give them a really long hug — don't let go until they start to wriggle away.

Role reversal: You will need to judge carefully whether this one is suitable for your child, but some children might enjoy a role reversal when it comes to separation anxiety, i.e. you being the one that doesn't want to let *them* go. You'll need to over-act this one and go really over the top to make them laugh. If your child likes this, they'll enjoy being the one that tells *you* that it's OK and you'll always come back.

Pushing: If your child is struggling with you leaving for work, then you could try adding a bit of playful interaction in before you go, for example get ready and open the door, and then say 'I don't think I'm quite ready to leave yet, I hope no one pushes me out of the door!' Then when your child pushes you out you can bounce back in saying you're not ready and you need more kisses/hugs.

Jewellery: I've linked from the resources page to a couple of bracelets that you can personalise with family names, to give a child a permanent reminder that they are part of the family. Some of the ones I've linked to have matching bracelets for parents and children. If bracelets aren't your thing, how about a pin badge? Something that your child can look at that reminds them you love them.

Exchanging objects: If you need to go away from your child, or they are going away from you (e.g. to school) then you could give each other a small object to 'look after', to help reassure your child that you will be back together later to give them back to each other. Or you could write a note to put in your child's lunchbox, or put a photo of you all together in their school bag.

ADOPTING A MUSICAL APPROACH

Charley Chatty and the Wiggly Worry Worm: A book by Sarah Naish, part of the William Wobbly series, this one addresses the issue of children who talk a lot to remind you that they are still there.

I keep a kiss in my pocket: On the resources page I've linked you to this sweet song about keeping a kiss in your pocket when you are separate from your child.

CAT McGILL

13
Who

Communication theme: Questions, turn-taking
Social/emotional theme: Attachment and bonding

Song lyrics

Who's got two blue eyes?
And soft brown hair up above?
And who's got a great big smiling mouth?
And who does mummy love?

Who's got two big feet?
With ten little wiggly toes!
And who's got a pair of flapping ears?
And who's got a cute little nose?

Who's got big strong arms?
And legs that jump and run?
And who's got a little cheeky chin?
And a very tickly tum!

Who's got two blue eyes?
And soft brown hair up above?
And who's got a great big smiling mouth?
And who does Mummy love?

Background

This song was inspired by the Theraplay measuring game I've described below, which I picked up on an introductory course I did just before we adopted Tickle. The theory behind the game is demonstrating that you are intensely interested in your child, which you show them by the time you spend measuring them, and how excited you are to see how big their ears/fingers/nose/smile has got. My children absolutely adore this game, not least because I use strawberry laces to measure them, and they get to eat each bit of lace after I've cut it. For this project, I wanted to write a song that could replicate that intense focus (though sadly this one doesn't involve strawberry laces), and I also wanted to incorporate an element of call and response, so that the child is involved in the interaction, to help support learning about turn-taking.

When I first sang this song to Tickle I didn't tell him what to expect, or what to do, but he picked it up instinctively, and answered each line with 'Me!' or by saying his name. You can draw each line out really slowly, taking your time over noticing each of the features; maybe count your child's toes together, or stroke their hair, give them an Eskimo kiss when you get to the nose part. You really want to lavish attention on to the child, as if they are the most fascinating thing in the whole world. As always, watch carefully for their reactions, and do back off if you think they are finding it too intense.

In normal speech you'd expect the pitch of your voice to rise at the end when you ask a question — and this is the case in Infant-Directed Speech (IDS) as well, except in the case of wh- questions. I've used this downwards contour for each of the lines that have 'who' in the question, though for the last line it goes back up to the key note at the end so that it sounds 'finished'.

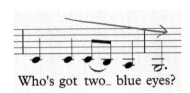
Who's got two_ blue eyes?

The second line of each verse doesn't have a wh- question, so I've used an upwards contour for the melody, partly to provide contrast and interest, and partly because in IDS this encourages the child to join in.

Developing language skills

In terms of Tickle's language skills, one thing I had to really practice with him when he first came to live with us was how he responded to the 'wh-' question words like who, what, and where. He didn't have an awful lot of language initially, so when I was trying to help him develop his conversational abilities I had to prompt him a lot with questions. For example, I would say 'What did you do at school today?' and he would (inevitably) answer 'Play'. Then I would say 'That sounds fun! Who did you play with?', to which the answer would usually be 'Cars'. So then I'd have to emphasise the 'who' in the question and give him some examples to show him what I meant: 'Oh great, cars are fun! But WHO did you play cars with? Did you play with another child, or a teacher, or on your own?' Gradually, over time this developed in to me asking the question 'What did you do at school today' and Tickle being able to answer 'I played cars with Barnaby'. It took several months of daily repetition to get to that stage though, so if it's not happening for you at the moment then do keep on gently trying.

Playing hide and seek and peekaboo are great ways of teaching your child about 'where'. Really over exaggerate your voice when you're asking '*Where* has Tickle gone?! *Where* could he be?' Pretend to look in all sort of places where you know they aren't, all the time narrating what you are doing: 'Is Tickle hiding under this chair? No! Then *where* could he be?'

For 'what' questions, how about having a bag of toys, and your child has to put their hand in and feel the different toys, as you ask them what they can feel. Or you could have different containers with different things in (e.g. shaving foam, jelly, water, sand) and they have to put their hands in and say what they think it is. To reinforce the language skills you could use a simple chant like 'What's in the box? What's in the box?'

Another good wh- word that doesn't make it in to the big five is 'which'. Which can be a useful word to help with choosing, and I usually use the Makaton sign alongside it as it is a really expressive sign that adds clarity to the word. To sign 'which' you need to make your hand in to a fist, with your little finger and your thumb sticking out, the same hand shape you would make if you were pretending to talk on the phone. Then hold you hand out so the back of your hand is facing upwards and your fingers are tucked underneath, and move it from side to side — this is the sign for which. When you are first introducing this sign, have two objects that you are choosing between and place them in front of you, so that when you move your hand between them the thumb points to one and the little finger points to the other — only roughly, you don't need to position them exactly. As you hand moves between the two objects it will help to reinforce the choice between the two things. Remember your child may make their choice by pointing, vocalising, or simply looking at the object that they want.

ADOPTING A MUSICAL APPROACH

Games and activities for getting to know you

For this chapter I've selected some games, songs, and activities that revolve around getting to know the child, being fascinated with them, and studying all the details of them as you might do with a brand new baby. This level of attention can be difficult for some children, so make sure you are receptive to the signals your child is giving you, and go slowly if you need to.

For less intense, more playful games have a look at chapter 4 (Hide and seek), and for a selection of focused, face-to-face activities see chapter 10 (I will love you). If you want more games around getting to know your body then have a look at chapter 2 (Any finer thing).

I've also included a few songs relating to question words, and linked up all the songs I've mentioned at catmcgill.uk/AAMA-resources for easy reference.

Drawing around your child: You can make a picture of part (or all) of your child by drawing around them on a large piece of paper. Maybe start with a hand or foot to gauge their reaction, and if you're doing a full body drawing do keep an eye on them to see how they are coping — a running commentary might be helpful to let them know whereabouts you are.

Tinfoil modelling: As an alternative to drawing, you can use ordinary tinfoil to make a model of your child's hand or foot. Get them to put their hand down and keep it still, then you can take your time over shaping the tinfoil over it — the idea being that you're really taking the time to study and concentrate on their hand while you're doing it. For children who aren't keen on touch this might provide an easier way in, as you're not touching them directly (although some children may not like the feel of tinfoil either).

Massage: If your child can tolerate it, massaging cream or lotion in to them can be a lovely soothing activity that will strengthen the bond between you. You can also talk to your child about their body as you're doing it, which again reinforces this idea that you are completely focused on them, for example 'I'm just rubbing cream in to your hand now, look at your long fingers! Here we go, all the way up this finger, round the back and over the fingernail... now let's do the next one...' ctc. You could also use rhymes like *Round and round the garden* or *This little piggy went to market* while you're doing it.

Measuring: My children *love* this game. It's very simple — you just measure different bits of them. You can do it with measuring tape or string, or (as we tend to do) strawberry laces. Measure some surprising things like the size of their smile, their ears, the length of their nose, etc, and show them 'Look how big your smile is!' Approached with curiosity and playfulness, this can be a really nurturing game.

Body lotion handprints: Apply some nice-smelling body lotion to your child's hand (or foot), and then get them to make a print on a piece of dark coloured paper. If you then shake some talcum powder on it, the powder will cling to the lotion so that when you blow or shake off the excess you will have a clear powder print of the hand or foot. For children who resist nurturing touch, this can be another way in as they are motivated by wanting to make a print. Obviously you can also do this with paint if your child doesn't mind getting a bit messy!

Decorating: If your child likes this sort of thing, decorating each other with temporary tattoos, glitter, or painting each other's nails can be a lovely nurturing activity to do together. You could also use face paint or make up.

Tony Chestnut: This is a great song for doing one to one, especially with quite a young child. You can chant it or sing it.

Tony Chestnut knows I love you
Tony knows, Tony knows
Tony Chestnut knows I love you
That's what Tony knows

ADOPTING A MUSICAL APPROACH

Start by singing the song slowly and touching the body parts that link up to the song:

Toe-knee chest-nut [head]
Nose eye love [put hands to heart] you [point]
Toe-knee nose
Toe-knee nose
Toe-knee chest-nut
Nose eye love you
That's what toe-knee nose

<u>Question words</u>

Who, What, When, Where, Why: Suitable for slightly older children, this funky song about the question words is quite entertaining, and shows how they all work together to answer questions.

Where oh where: I mentioned this game in a previous chapter, but I've added it here because it's good for practising question vocabulary. The game starts off as a hide and seek game, where a toy (or a person) is hiding, and the seekers all sing (to the tune of *Bobby Shaftoe*):

Where oh where oh where is Mummy? [or whoever is hiding]
Where oh where oh where is Mummy?
Where oh where oh where is Mummy?
Where has Mummy gone?

You can then expand on this to include other questions words, like 'What oh what is Mummy doing?' or 'Why oh why is Mummy hiding?'

One, two, three, four, five: This well-known nursery rhyme has a couple of good wh- question words in: why, and which. You can make up extra verses with different animals and different body parts if you like.

I look in the mirror: I found a poem (linked from my resources page) that is about looking in the mirror and seeing different bits of your face ('I looked in the mirror, and what did I see…') which I thought it might be quite fun to do with a child, sat in front of a mirror, but using a different toy each time, and using the questions 'what do I see' as a prompt to describe the feature of the toy. You could also adapt it for 'who' questions like this:

I looked in the mirror, and WHO did I see?
I saw Tickle looking back at me!
He gave me a wave and he blew me a kiss
Then he made a really silly face, just like this…

Then your child makes a silly face in to the mirror and you have to copy it.

As long as you love me: A golden oldie from the Backstreet Boys, this song has a chorus full of question words, and is suitable for using with slightly older children. It could also be a good opportunity to start a conversation about the rest of the lyrics, and what message you think the singers are trying to get over.

There are plenty of other pop songs with questions in — from *What's the frequency Kenneth?* to *How deep is your love* so consider this your excuse to build up a huge playlist and get singing along, all in the name of language development!

14
The River

Communication theme: Soothing and calming
Social/emotional theme: Change

Song lyrics

The river runs against the wind
Night by night and day by day
Watch the leaf that's fallen in
Drifting down along the way

Everything's the same, but everything's changed

Crystal water flowing clear
Leaf is whisked around the bend
Swirling, whirling far and near
Carried on to journey's end

Everything's the same, but everything's changed

Six bulrushes standing proud
Softly shed their downy coat
Floating lightly as a cloud
Comes to rest on leafy boat

Everything's the same, but everything's changed

Winter segues into spring
The river runs its merry way
Twisting, turning, tumbling

CAT McGILL

Night by night and day by day

Everything's the same, but everything's changed
Everything's the same, but everything's changed

Background

This song started out life trying to be *Little fish's Big Journey*; I was thinking about using the metaphor of a leaf floating down the river to talk about how sometimes things change, even though they still look more or less the same from the outside. However, it wasn't really doing the job I wanted it to do as a song addressing the topic of life story, so I decided it was better suited as a more abstract lullaby about change.

I went for a walk one afternoon looking for inspiration for songs, and happened to wander along past a river. It was quite a windy day, and I noticed that the wind was blowing ripples on the surface of the water in one direction, but that underneath the surface I could still see things floating down in the other direction, pulled by the current. As I watched it, fascinated, the first line of the song floated in to my head: 'The river runs against the wind'. The rest of the song didn't come quite as easily, and took quite a lot more walking, and a lot of looking at rivers and ponds, and noticing things that I saw. Luckily for me, I was writing the song as winter was indeed segueing in to spring, and there were lots of things to look at, not least the lovely downy bulrushes that were shedding their fluff everywhere.

Although the changing of the seasons didn't end up being central to the narrative of this song, it was one of the topics I was considering for my song about change. One thing we have really noticed in our family is that the shifting of the season can often bring about a shift in behaviour, with certain behaviours and issues being more prevalent at some times of year than at others. For example, Tickle hardly ever mentions his foster carers (he was only with them a very short time) but around the anniversary of when he was taken in to care their names will pop up in conversation, and he will ask to look at photos of them. There is *something* in his environment that is triggering this memory — whether it's the light changing, the leaves on the trees, or what I don't know.

The communication theme I've chosen for this chapter is soothing and calming. This is less about your child's ability to communicate, and more about how you can communicate to them in a soothing and calming way to encourage them to rest and relax. I've deliberately used a very repetitive melody in this song, where the second two lines of each verse are an exact melodic repeat of the first two lines. This also gives the effect of the melody gently going up and down, up and down, which is really calming for the nervous system. The narrative of the song is very slow; there's no real story to it, it just wends its way along gently like a river, and the gaps and pauses between each line stretch it out even more.

This is also a technique I use to help settle Tickle at night time if I'm telling him a story — drawing out the vowels in each word to make them longer, and introducing slight pauses after each sentence, which can gradually get longer as you go on. As you are increasing the pauses between sentences or words it may help to keep a face to face connection with your child, so they can continue to pick up the safety cues from your social engagement system. Most people will naturally lower their voice when they are trying to speak in a calming way, and make it gentle and sing-songy.

CAT McGILL

Lullabies

In this chapter I've decided to focus on songs that can help sooth or relax a child. You might want to couple some of these with something like a little massage, or some nice scented candles, but you'll need to try things out to find what your child finds relaxing — not all children will like to be touched for example. I have included a couple of songs below that you will know, but I've mainly tried to find ones that you may not have come across. All the songs and any specific resources from the suggestions below are linked from my website catmcgill.uk/AAMA-resources.

Dream Angus: This folk song was recorded by Jackie Oates, and is the first track on her Lullabies album. The whole album is beautiful and I can really recommend it for a soothing, calming listen.

Jesu, Joy of Man's Desiring: I haven't included much classical music in my recommendations but I've included a few in this chapter. This one is Tickle's favourite bedtime song, and he always requests it to go to sleep to.

Sleep: Sleep by Eric Whittaker is another one on our bedtime playlist. It's a modern classical piece, beautiful and soothing.

Canon in D for strings: Better known as Pachelbel's Canon, this piece of music is supposed to be one of the most calming ever written. I remember hearing once about the tempo of the music being close to the human resting heart rate but I have no idea how true that is.

Go to sleep little baby: This American lullaby was featured in the film *O Brother Where Art Thou*, and it has a really beautiful gentle rocking rhythm to it.

Twinkle twinkle: Everyone knows this classic nursery rhyme, but did you know it started off as a poem, and there are more verses than you probably realised?

ADOPTING A MUSICAL APPROACH

Hush little baby: This is another of Tickle's most requested lullabies. Remember you don't have to have the voice of an angel to sing to your child — they like it because it's you.

Cradle song: Also known as *Brahm's Lullaby*, I'm sure you'll recognise the tune to this, even if you don't know the words (I didn't either). I've linked you up to a really lovely version of this from my website and I'm looking forward to adding it to my repertoire of bedtime songs.

Up the wooden hill to Bedfordshire: A song by Vera Lynn, this might be a nice alternative for an older child who has grown out of nursery rhymes but would still like a song at bedtime.

Everything possible: This is a beautiful song by Roy Bailey, with a lovely message to it: 'You can be anybody you want to be, you can love whomever you will'. It also explicitly mentions LGBT relationships if that's something important in your family.

Bonny at Morn: A beautiful Northumbrian lullaby. The words are written in northern dialect so some children may find them hard to understand.

A dream is a wish your heart makes: A Disney lullaby from the film *Cinderella*. Some other great lullabies from Disney are *Baby Mine* from *Dumbo*, *La La Lu* from *Lady and the Tramp*, and *Stay Awake* from *Mary Poppins*. I also always loved *Love Goes On*, from Disney's *Robin Hood*.

CAT McGILL

ADOPTING A MUSICAL APPROACH

To my readers: Thank you for reading Adopting a Musical Approach*! I really hope you've found it useful, and that you've enjoyed listening to the songs — and hopefully dancing along too.*

I always love to hear from people who've enjoyed my books, so please do visit my website catmcgill.uk, or you can find me on Twitter or Facebook @folkycat.

If you've enjoyed the book, I'd really appreciate if you could leave me a short review on Amazon or Goodreads — it can make a really big difference to independent authors like me, and helps me get my work out to even more people who need it.

I'd like to thank my wonderful family; my husband for slipping seamlessly into the role of primary carer so I can concentrate on work, and my children for putting up with me always needing to be off doing things at funny times of day. Thank you to Fairy for lending your beautiful voice to the album recording, and Tickle for adding some of your own unique joy — and to both of you for being the guinea pigs for all the songs I've written! I know I can always rely on you to tell me if it's no good.

I have to give an honourable mention here to my producer Pete Ord, who not only helped me write some of the tracks on the album, but supported me through the whole process and turned it round in super quick time. Also my editor Sarah Giles, who calmly accepted that I wanted to write and publish a book inside three months, and had a full copy edit back to me within 48 hours of receiving the draft manuscript. My good friend Ollie King took the fabulous photos you see on the book cover, and the artwork was done by the very talented Katy Coope, who has been nothing but professional and patient with me as I keep adding 'just once more thing'.

For more information about me and my work, and to download your free copy of What's Next For Unicorns? — a laugh out loud account of Fairy's early years — please visit catmcgill.uk

Also by Cat McGill:

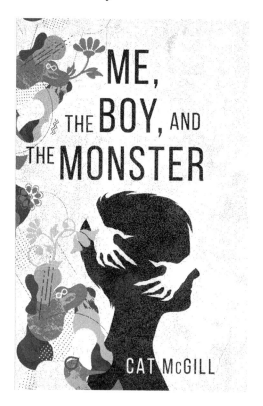

Me, the Boy, and The Monster is a personal, thoughtful, and touching tribute to a family's journey through the world of adoption and trauma. McGill has a background in developmental psychology and uses this to great effect; the theory sections of *MTBTM* are relevant, researched, and related to real-life examples from McGill's own experience with her adopted son. This book goes beyond the tired cliché of 'attachment' however, pulling together relevant strands of many different psychological theories and disciplines, all of which is juxtaposed against heart-wrenching and emotional accounts taken from McGill's own blog, giving the reader a unique and personal insight in to the day to day struggles of her family.

Read on for a preview...

'This isn't just a book for people before they adopt; this is also a book for adopters. There were so many things you said that resonated so clearly with my experience. You articulate the concepts beautifully and the personal illustration from your life, so generously included, brings it to life and makes it real.'

— *Adoptive parent*

'I LOVE IT! It's written in a really easy-to-understand way, without too much jargon, and the technical stuff is explained in a clear way.'

— *Adoptive parent*

'Your description of The Monster is a real insight into trauma and its effects on the children. I really gained an understanding and even recognised some traits in our 17-month-old. I appreciate the honesty you have included with your examples – letting the reader know what works/doesn't work and that you have to change your approach as the child develops/heals.'

— *Adoptive parent*

Introduction

Let me introduce you to the people in my family. There's me – I'm the mum; Husband – he's the dad. There's Fairy – a funny, empathetic 10-year-old, and my daughter by birth. And then there's Tickle. A sweet, funny, and extremely traumatised little boy, who is my 7-year-old son by adoption.

And then, there's 'The Monster'. The Monster lives inside Tickle, and his job is to protect Tickle from danger, at all costs. The Monster makes fairly frequent appearances in our lives, as he is a little oversensitive when it comes to thinking that Tickle is unsafe. The Monster was quite scary for a while, but these days I think of him as something akin to Sully from Monsters Inc., or one of the ones off Monster Munch packets. Big, fluffy, turquoise… a little misguided, very loyal, and doing his best to keep Tickle safe in the only way he knows how.

I should say at this point that the concept of The Monster is in no way a scientific theory; it is not a piece of researched or peer-reviewed academic work, but a metaphor from my own thoughts, used as a way of making sense of things. For my family, it's proved useful to help us start to understand Tickle and his behaviour – particularly for Fairy. She obviously knows very little of Tickle's early life, but using 'The Monster' we have been able to explain about trauma, and the effect it is having on Tickle in a way that's allowed her to separate out Tickle's behaviour from who he is as a person. She can hate The Monster, but still love Tickle, and that has been really important for her. And for me too, if I'm honest. I don't hate The Monster, because I understand why he's there, but there have been many times where it's been beneficial for me to have him separate from Tickle in my mind.

Tickle shouldn't need a 'Monster'. No child should. Children should have parents that keep them safe. Parents who teach them how to react to different situations, how to pick yourself up when you've fallen over, what to do when you feel sad. Children shouldn't need to worry about where their food is coming from, or if someone is going to take it away. Children shouldn't need to worry that adults are going to hurt them. Children should always have someone to rely on, unquestionably, unconditionally. At the very root of everything, it's all about survival.

In some ways, The Monster 'grew' because Tickle didn't have those things. The world is a very big and frightening place, and when you don't have a secure and confident person to help you navigate it, you need *something* to make sense of it all. In this metaphor, The Monster is a part of Tickle – living in the primitive, survival part of Tickle's brain, which we as parents spend time soothing in babies and young children. The Monster has grown out of the part of the brain that makes a baby cry because it's hungry, or needs changing, or wants a cuddle. It's there to help a child survive, to help them connect with the adults around them, to build their place in the world and start to understand how to get their needs met. But for Tickle, part of that equation was missing – the part with the consistent, unconditional, responsive adult. As a result, The Monster was the only thing that Tickle had to help him survive. The Monster grew, and he depended on it. He didn't know any different.

However noble The Monster's intentions are, the fact is it operates on a skewed version of the world as we know it – one where adults aren't reliable, where loud noises can mean danger, and where you don't know if you are safe. The Monster is childish and primitive, his only objective is to keep Tickle safe, and he will do whatever it needs to do in order to achieve this. Sometimes The Monster gets Tickle to run away from things. Sometimes The Monster makes Tickle shout, scream, or talk nonsense at the top of his voice, to drown out the things in his head. Sometimes The Monster hits us, headbutts, bites, kicks, spits, or pushes us – me, Husband, or Fairy.

Our journey with Tickle and his Monster is still very much at the beginning. They've lived with us for nearly two years as I sit writing this, and we are discovering more about both of them every day. I haven't yet worked out all the answers, or discovered the magic wand that will make all our problems go away(!), but I do feel like we have reached a place where we are starting to understand what's going on. That probably doesn't sound particularly momentous to you, but I can

ME, THE BOY, AND THE MONSTER

assure you, having spent the first year in total chaos, 'starting to understand' feels like an achievement worth marking!

There is a wonderful quote about trauma that I found in one of the many articles I have read since starting the adoption process, and it is this:

'This is not about something you think or something you figure out. This is about your body, your organism, having been reset to interpret the world as a terrifying place and yourself as being unsafe. And it has nothing to do with cognition… you can say to people, "You shouldn't feel that way," or, "You're not a bad person," or, "It wasn't your fault." And people say, "I know that, but I feel that it is."'
                                                    – Bessel Van Der Kolk

For me, that is the essence of The Monster. You can know, logically, that you are safe, but the feelings are still there. The Monster is still there. Our challenge currently is where we go from here.

In those early days, my biggest dream was that with my undying love and commitment Tickle would start to feel as though he's safe and cared for. I suspect this is something a lot of adoptive parents can relate to – the desperate need to heal your child with your love.

I've found the reality to be rather different. After nearly two years I am relying much more on the cognitive understanding than I ever thought I would; trying to find a balance between thinking and feeling, between his emotions and mine, between Tickle's need to hit things and Fairy's need for it not to be her. Love plays a part, but it's only one piece of the puzzle.

I have learned a lot during this time, and if I'm honest, very little of the preparation I did during the adoption process had me ready for what we have faced. This came as quite a shock, as I really thought I was prepared. I already had a child, I'm a qualified teacher, I have worked for years with children with special needs, traumatised and vulnerable children and adults, studied psychology, and read virtually every adoption book I could get my hands on. I can be realistic, and I know that you're never *really* prepared for parenthood in whatever form it takes – but this has gone far beyond the initial shock to the system. This has been an intrinsic lack of understanding regarding the extent of Tickle's trauma, both from ourselves and from the professionals who were supposed to be supporting us, and at times a complete lack of willingness of the professionals to acknowledge it. It has been a fight to get the support services we need in place. I got to a point around 18 months in where I seriously thought I couldn't go on any more.

This book is a mixture of information, and personal reflections taken from my blog, designed to give an insight in to our lives with Tickle, and put all the information into some context. I have tried to mix it up, so you get a theoretical chapter, followed by a chapter giving some personal insights on how understanding the theory has impacted on my parenting. What I'm aiming for is to write the book I would have liked to read – either before becoming Tickle's mother or at the very least soon after we'd met him. I'd like to dedicate it to all the other adopters out there who have children with live-in 'Monsters' – know you are not alone.

*****

To order your copy of *Me, the Boy, and The Monster* go to catmcgill.uk/publications or search on Amazon or iBooks.

About the Author

Hello! Thank you for reading my book. I'm Cat, I'm a musician and writer, and a mum to two children with special needs. I'm autistic myself as well, though I wasn't diagnosed until my late thirties. Ever since I can remember I've been fascinated by people — their relationships with one another, what makes them tick, how they learn, etc. I decided when I was nine that I was going to study psychology at university, and — never having been able to make my mind up whether I wanted to be a musician or a psychologist — I have bounced between the two ever since.

Adopting a Musical Approach was born from my day job of using music to help support children with profound and multiple learning difficulties, and wanting to see how I could apply my skills from there to help my son, and other adopted children. I had great feedback from the adoption community from my first book *Me, the Boy, and The Monster* so I've taken a similar approach with *AAMA*; a mix of the theory and the practical, of psychology and real-life experience.

I hope you've enjoyed the book, and I'd love to hear how you got on with the songs and games! Keep in touch on social media @folkycat.

45003995R00099

Printed in Poland
by Amazon Fulfillment
Poland Sp. z o.o., Wrocław